Houghton Mifflin Science

DiscoveryWorks

HOUGHTON MIFFLIN

Boston • Atlanta • Dallas • Denver • Geneva, Illinois • Palo Alto • Princeton

Authors

William Badders
Elementary Science Teacher
Cleveland Public Schools
Cleveland, OH

Lowell J. Bethel
Professor of Science Education
The University of Texas at Austin
Austin, TX

Victoria Fu
Professor of Child Development
and Early Childhood Education
Virginia Polytechnic Institute and
State University
Blacksburg, VA

Donald Peck
Director (retired)
The Center for Elementary Science
Fairleigh Dickinson University
Madison, NJ

Carolyn Sumners
Director of Astronomy and Physical Sciences
Houston Museum of Natural Science
Houston, TX

Catherine Valentino
Author-in-Residence, Houghton Mifflin
West Kingston, RI

Consulting Author

R. Mike Mullane
Astronaut, retired
Albuquerque, NM

Acknowledgements appear on page H28, which
constitutes an extension of this copyright page.

Printed in the U. S. A.

ISBN 0-618-00630-3

1 2 3 4 5 6 7 8 9 10 RRD 08 07 06 05 04 03 02 01 00 99

CONTENTS

THINK LIKE A SCIENTIST

THINK
LIKE A SCIENTIST

Spinning Tops

Observe

To think like a scientist, **observe** the things around you. Everything you hear and see is a clue about how the world works.

Two friends, Lisa and Carl, are spinning tops. They spin their tops at the same time. Each time, Carl's top is first to stop spinning. Why did this happen?

Ask a Question

As you observe, you may see that some things happen over and over. **Ask questions** about such things.

Lisa spins her top on a smooth floor. Carl spins his on a rug. Lisa wonders, does the kind of floor make Carl's top stop first? What do you think?

Make a Hypothesis

Suppose you have an idea about why something happens. You make a **hypothesis**, or a guess based on your idea.

Lisa has an idea about what made Carl's top stop first. She thinks it might be the bumpy rug. How can she find out?

Plan and Do a Test

After you make a hypothesis, **plan** how to **test** it. Then carry out your plan.

Lisa and Carl test the idea. Carl spins his top on the smooth table. Lisa spins her top on the bumpy cement.

Record What Happens

You need to observe your test carefully. Then **record**, or write down, what happens.

Lisa sees that her top slows down and stops sooner. She writes down what happened. What does she write?

Draw Conclusions

Think about reasons why something happened as it did. Then **draw conclusions**.

Lisa thinks about the test.
She decides that bumps cause a top to stop sooner. You try it!

Reading to Learn

Before You Read

1. **Look** at the pictures.
2. **Read** the words.
3. **Read** the title.
4. **Look** at the **new words**.

Comparing Plants

The same parts of different plants look different. You see fruit on one plant. You see flowers on two plants. The spruce tree doesn't have flowers. It has cones. Both **cones** and flowers make seeds that grow into new plants.

A12  KINDS OF LIVING THINGS

Scientists read to have fun and to learn. You can, too! Just follow these steps.

The trees grow very tall. The rosebush and sunflower don't grow as tall. The sunflower has big, flat leaves. The spruce tree has thin, pointed leaves. This kind of leaf is called a **needle**. How are other plants different from these?

Reading Check **Draw a picture** of two different plants. Tell how their parts are different.

LESSON 3 RESOURCE  A13

While You Read

1. **Read** the words carefully.
2. **Look** at the pictures again.
3. **Ask** for help if you need it.

After You Read

1. **Tell** what you have learned.
2. **Show** what you have learned.

SAFETY

Wear your goggles when your teacher tells you.

Handle materials carefully.

Never put things into your mouth.

Wash your hands after every activity.

Always tell an adult if you are hurt.

Be kind to living things.

Clean up spills.

Save resources and materials to use again.

Throw out materials you can't use again.

Kinds of Living Things

Theme: Systems

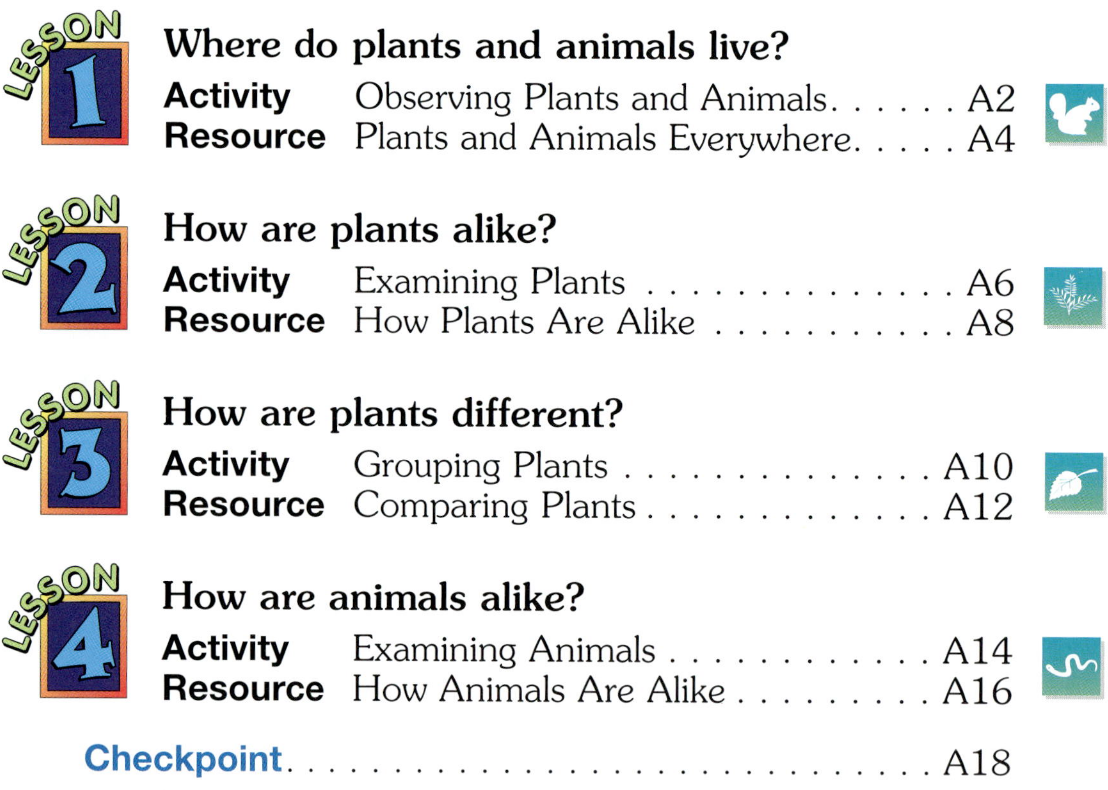

Where do plants and animals live?

Activity

Observing Plants and Animals

What You Need

 crayons

Science Notebook

1. Take a walk with your class. **Look at** plants and animals.

2. **Draw** the plants you see. **Write** or **tell** about where you see the plants.

3. **Draw** the animals you see. **Write** or **tell** about what the animals are doing.

Think! **How are plants and animals different from each other?**

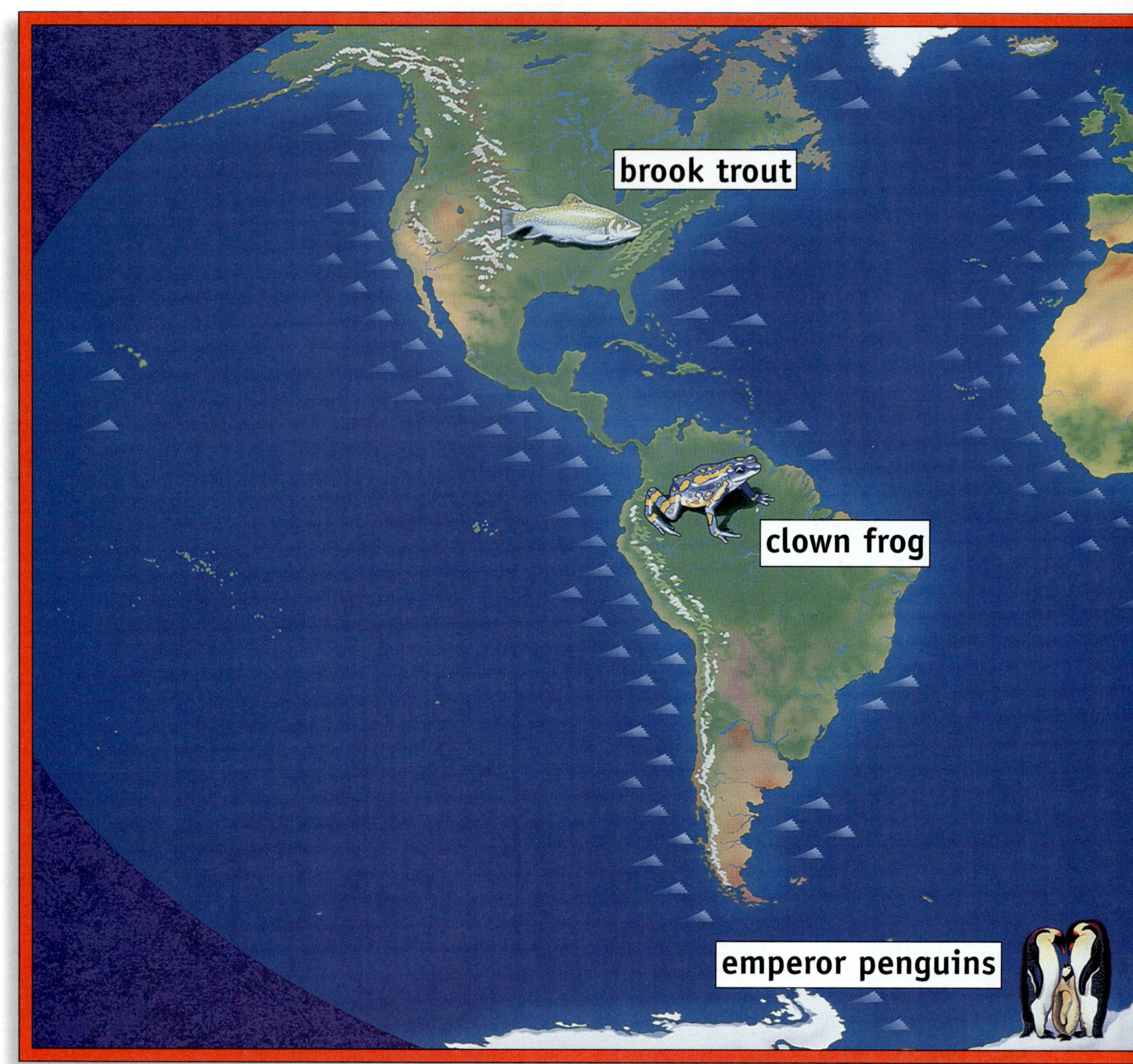

Plants and Animals Everywhere

There are many kinds of plants and animals. They live where they can get what they need to stay alive. They live on the land, in the water, and in the air. They live in your home. Plants and animals live almost everywhere on the earth.

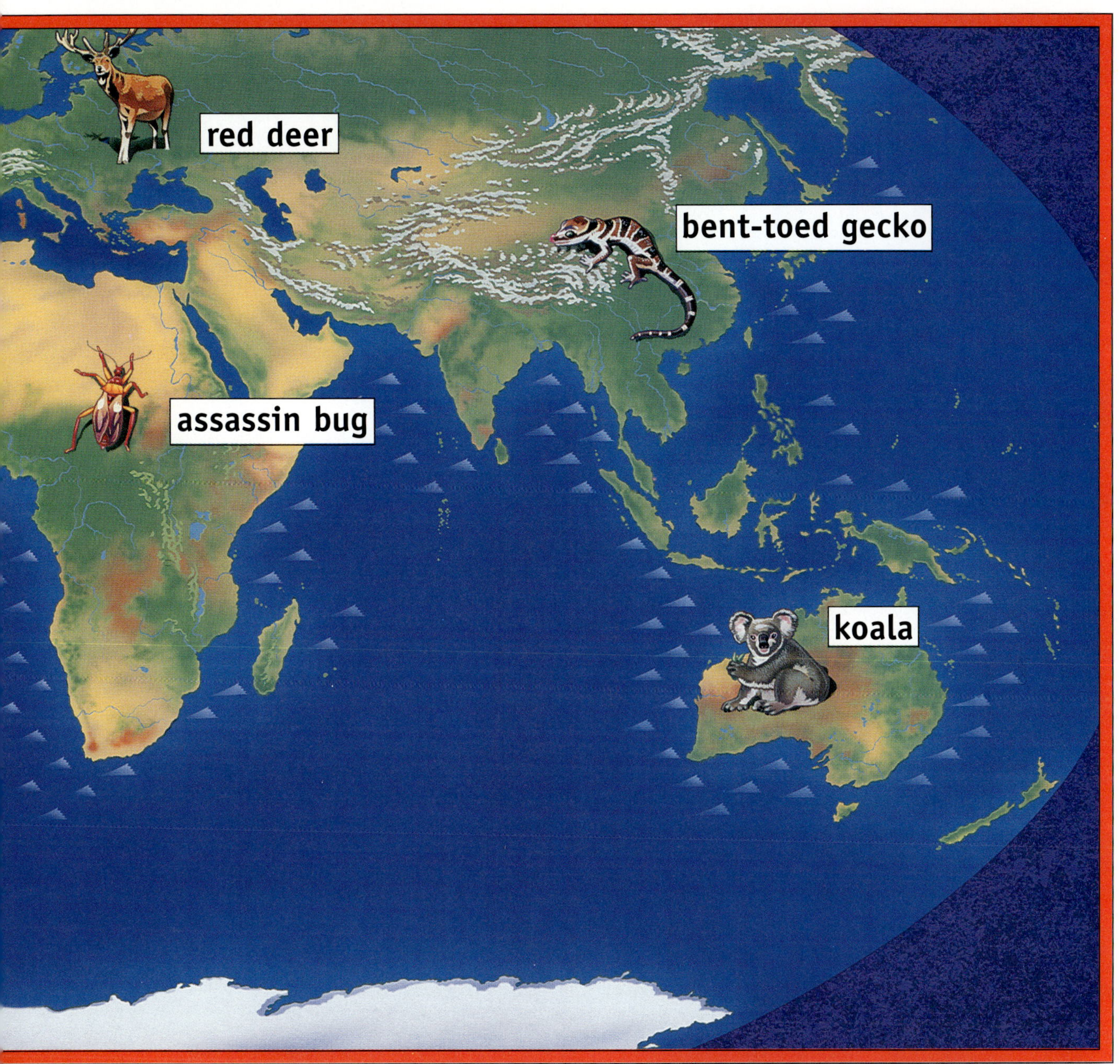

A different kind of animal is shown on each continent. Each place is different. Some places are hot. Others are cold. Some places are wet. Others are dry. That's why different animals and plants live in each place.

Reading Check **Tell about** some of the places where different animals live.

How are plants alike?

Activity
Examining Plants

What You Need

different live plants

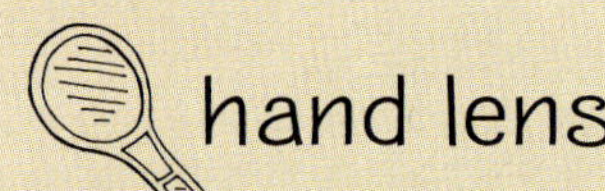
hand lens

Science Notebook

1. **Look at** different plants. Use a hand lens to **look at** the different parts.

2. **Look for** ways that the plants are all the same.

3 **Record** your findings.

Think! How are all these plants alike?

Internet Field Trip

Visit **www.eduplace.com** to learn more about plants.

How Plants Are Alike

Plants are living things. Plants need water, light, and air to grow. Plants stay in one place unless moved. Most plants have roots, stems, and leaves. Many have flowers. **Flowers** make seeds that grow into new plants.

Roots grow down in soil. Roots take in water. Most stems grow above ground. **Stems** carry water from the roots to other plant parts. Leaves grow on a stem or up from the roots. **Leaves** use sunlight to make food for the plant.

Reading Check **Write a story** about a plant. Tell what each part does. How is it like other plants?

LESSON 3

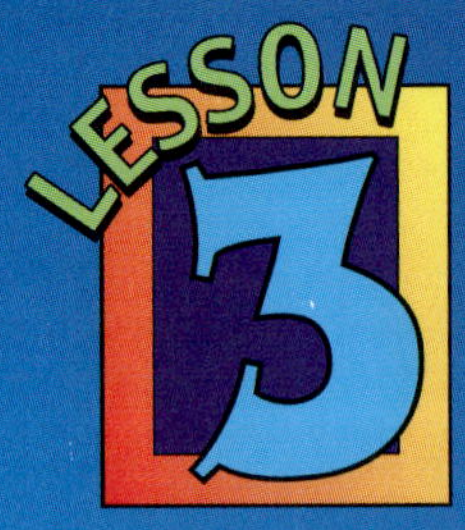

How are plants different?

Activity

Grouping Plants

What You Need

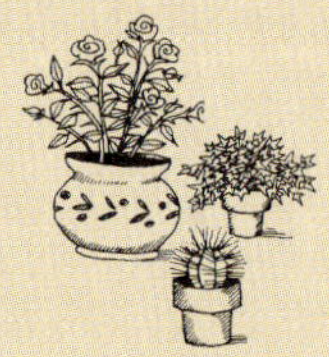
different live plants

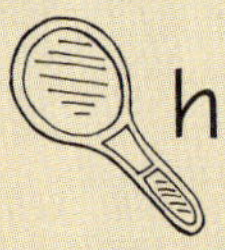
hand lens

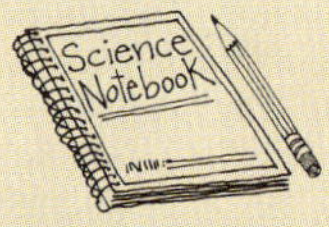

Science Notebook

1. **Look at** the plants and their parts. **Talk about** how each part looks.

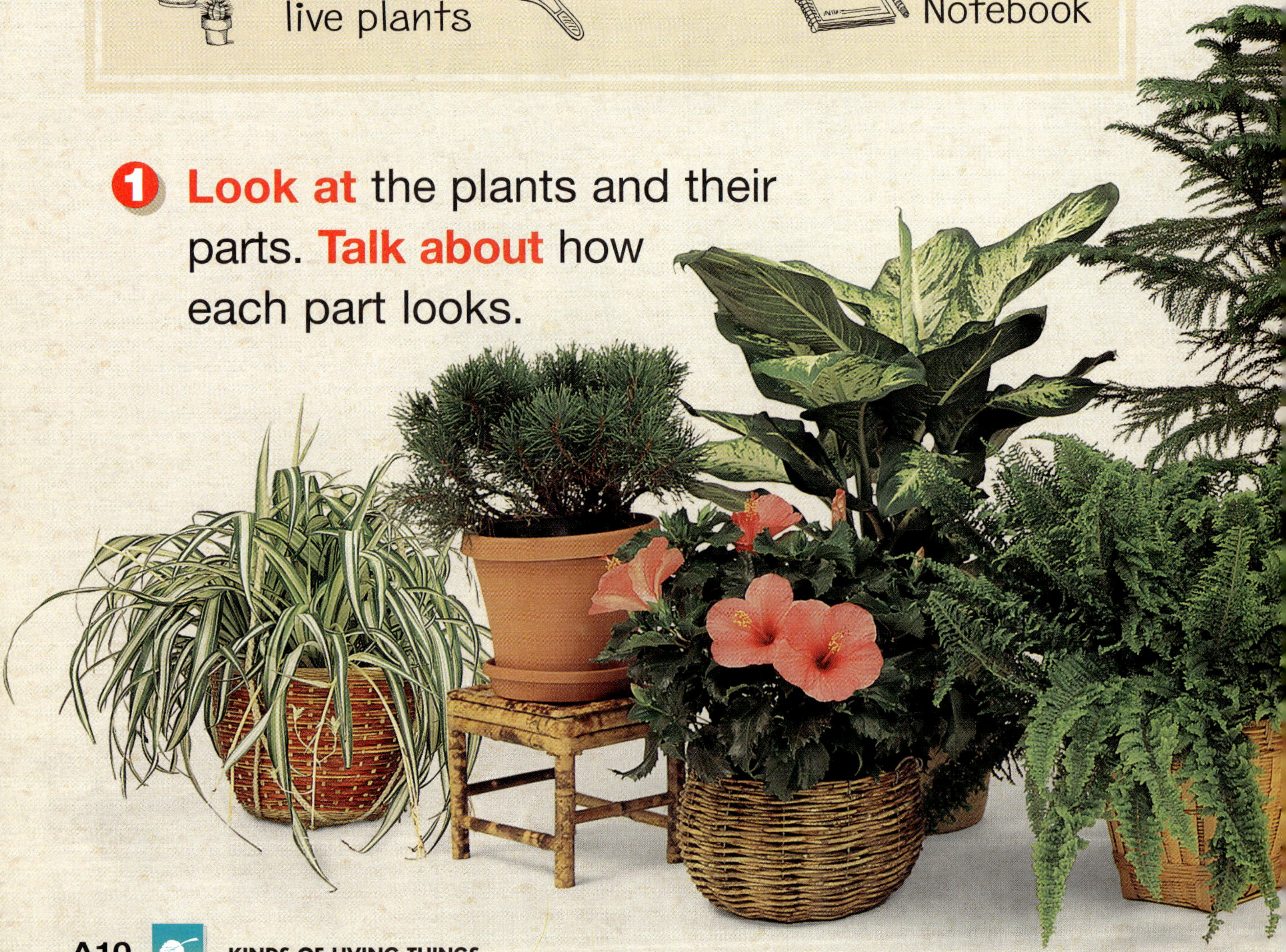

2 **Sort** the plants into groups.

3 **Make a tally chart** to record your groups.

Using Math

Grouping Plants		
Group	Tally	Total

Think! What makes one plant different from another?

Comparing Plants

The same parts of different plants look different. You see fruit on one plant. You see flowers on two plants. The spruce tree doesn't have flowers. It has cones. Both **cones** and flowers make seeds that grow into new plants.

The trees grow very tall. The rosebush and sunflower don't grow as tall. The sunflower has big, flat leaves. The spruce tree has thin, pointed leaves. This kind of leaf is called a **needle**. How are other plants different from these?

Reading Check **Draw a picture** of two different plants. Tell how their parts are different.

How are animals alike?

Activity
Examining Animals

What You Need

different live animals

Science Notebook

1 **Look at** different animals.

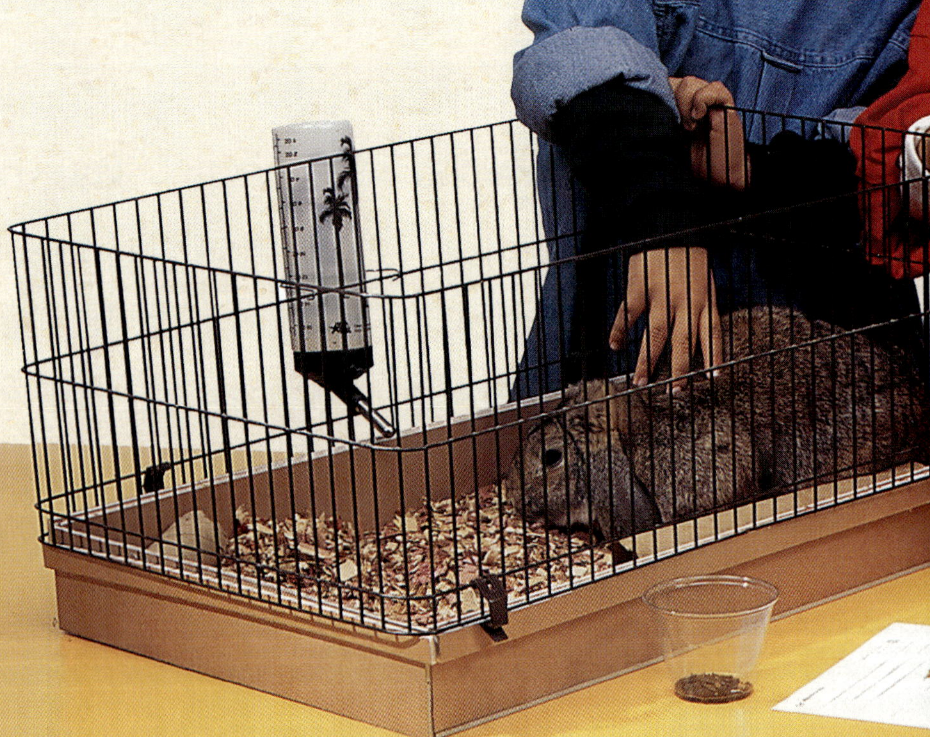

2. **Look for** ways that the animals are all the same.

3. **Record** your findings.

Think! How are all these animals alike?

> **Find Out More!**
>
> Measure the mass of a baby animal every week for four weeks. Record the mass. What changes do you see? Do other baby animals change in the same way?

How Animals Are Alike

Animals are living things. They are alike in many ways. All animals have a body covering. They all need food, water, and air.

Animals can move. They move to find food. They also move to get away from danger.

Animals need homes. They need homes for shelter. They need homes for safety. All kinds of animals can make baby animals.

Many kinds of animals live in this swamp. How are these animals alike?

Reading Check **Write a list** of things that all animals need to live. Do you need the same things?

CHECKPOINT

Word Power

If you need help, turn to the pages shown in blue.

Match a word with a picture. (A8, A12–A13)

cone flower needle

1.  **2.**  **3.** 

Use these words to fill in the blanks.

Roots Stems leaves

4. The plant parts that make food are _____. (A8–A9)

5. _____ carry water to other plant parts. (A8–A9)

6. _____ grow down in soil. (A8–A9)

Solving Science Problems

Your class wants to have a plant sale. Use the questions below to help you plan. Talk about each question. Then decide how to answer it.

1. What kinds of plants will you sell?

2. What size plants will you sell?

3. How will you care for your plants before the sale?

People Using Science

Zoologist

Zoologists study animals. Some zoologists work in zoos. They take care of animals' needs.

They design homes for animals. Some homes have trees. Others have rocks. Homes can be wet or dry.

Why is this a good home for a tree kangaroo? How might a seal's home look?

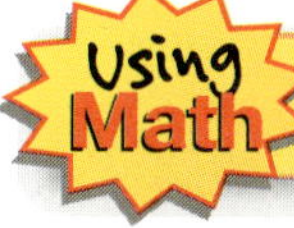

Find a Pattern

Look at the patterns of plants and animals. Draw what comes next.

1.  ____________

2.  ____________

3.  ____________

How are body coverings different?

Examining Body Coverings

What You Need

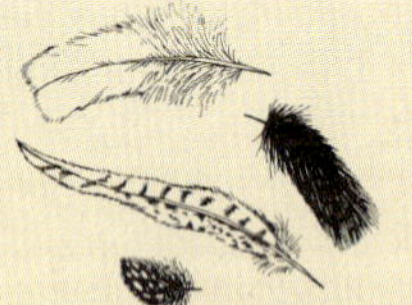
feathers of different birds

hand lens

dried fish scales

Science Notebook

1. Use a hand lens to **look at** your skin. **Draw** what you see.

2. Use the hand lens to **look at** fish scales. **Draw** what you see.

3. **Look at** feathers. **Draw** what you see.

4. **Compare** your drawings.

Think! How are skin, fish scales, and feathers alike and different?

Body Coverings

All animals have a body covering. Many are covered by **skin**. Some have a covering over their skin. Look at the many body coverings. Find hair. It can be long or short. It can be thick or thin. Thick **hair** is called fur.

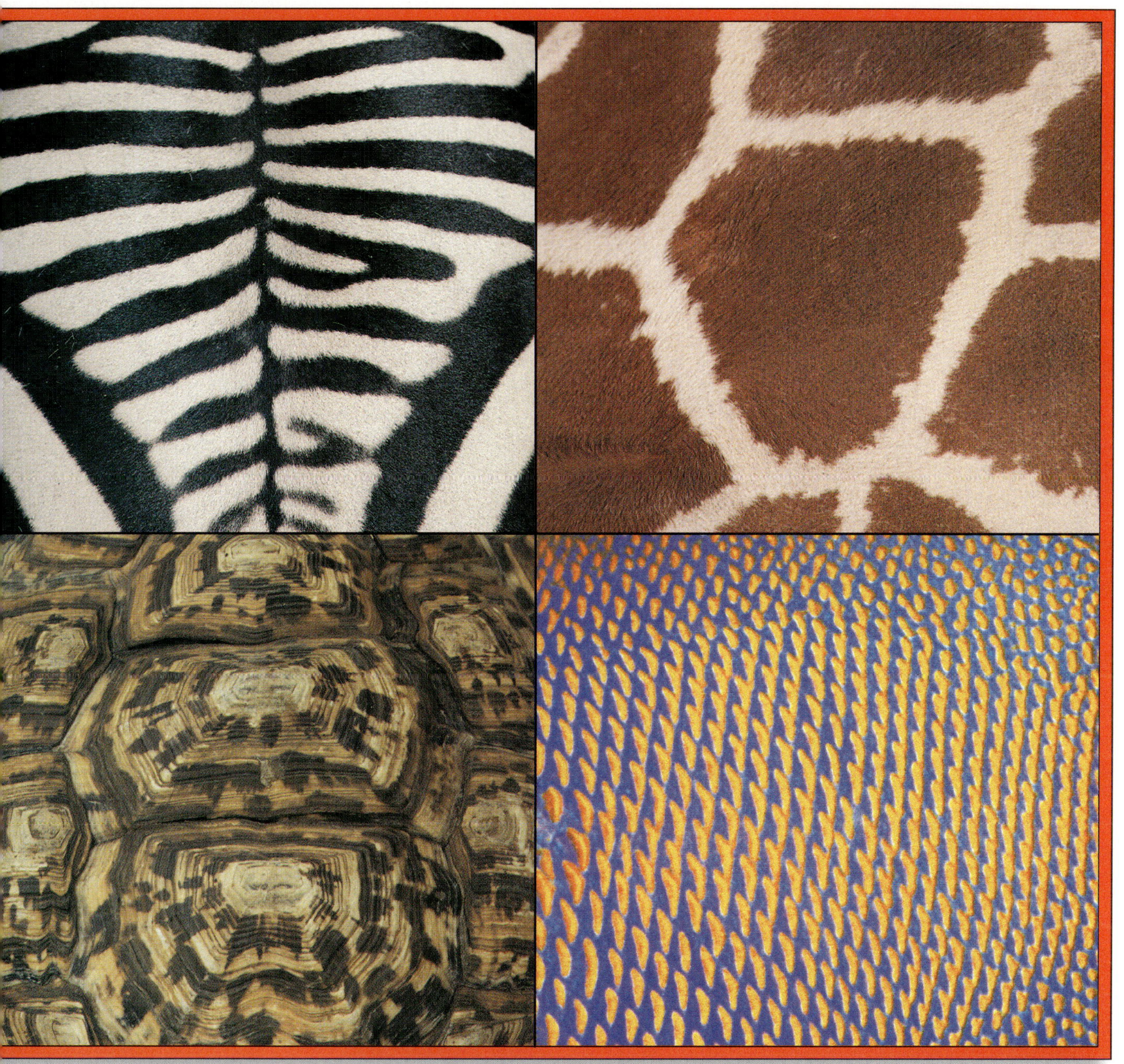

Look for feathers. **Feathers** cover a bird's skin. Look for scales. **Scales** are thin and flat. Fish and snakes have scales. Now find a shell. Most shells are hard. Turtles have shells. Do you see quills? Quills are thick and pointy. What animals have these body coverings?

Body coverings help animals meet their needs. Hair helps keep a dog warm. Feathers help keep a bird dry. Skin helps keep animals cool.

Body coverings can also help keep animals safe. Scales help keep a fish from getting cut. A shell gives a turtle a place to hide.

Body coverings can also help animals move. Feathers help birds fly through the air. Scales help snakes crawl on the ground.

Body coverings can be many colors. What colors do you see? Colors help you tell animals apart.

Reading Check **Draw** two different animals. Tell how their body coverings are different.

How are animal homes different?

Making a Goldfish Home

What You Need

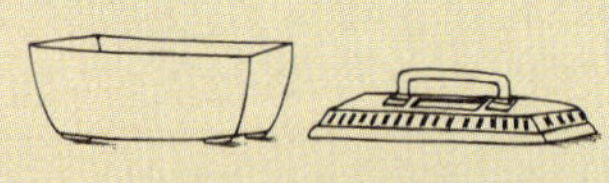
clear plastic container

container of water

assorted aquarium materials

Science Notebook

1. **Plan** a home you can make for a goldfish. **Record** your plan.
2. Make your goldfish home.
3. **Predict** where the goldfish will go when you put it in the home. **Record** your prediction.

4 Put a goldfish in the home.
Record where the goldfish goes.

Making a Goldfish Home
Plan
Prediction
Where the goldfish goes

Think! How does a goldfish use the things in its home for shelter and safety?

Find Out More!

How do other animals use things in their homes for shelter and safety? Ask questions. Make a plan to find answers. Share your findings.

Some Animal Homes

All animals need homes. Some animals have homes in water. Some animals make homes in trees. Other animals make their homes underground. Some animals carry their homes with them. Other animals share homes.

A home gives an animal shelter. A **shelter** helps keep an animal safe. It protects the animal from bad weather. Look at the homes in the picture. How are these homes different?

What kinds of animals might live in each home? Turn the page to find out.

Hornets, weavers, and bats live in these homes. The hornets make their nest from paper. They make the paper from chewed-up plants.

The birds make a nest of grass. The nest helps keep the baby birds safe. Bats don't build a home. They use a cave for shelter.

big brown bats

Some animals use their homes to store food. The hornets use their nest to store food.

Your home gives you shelter. It helps keep you safe. Do people use plants to build homes? How else is your home like an animal's home?

Reading Check **Write a story** about two animals. Tell how they use plants for shelters.

How do mouth parts help an animal eat?

Activity
Looking at Teeth

1. Take a bite of a carrot stick. **Record** which teeth you used.

2. Use a mirror to **look at** those teeth. **Record** what they look like.

3. Chew the carrot stick. **Record** which teeth you used.

4. Use the mirror to **look at** those teeth. **Record** what they look like.

Think! How are teeth used for biting different from teeth used for chewing?

Comparing Mouth Parts

All animals need food to live. Some animals eat plants. Many animals eat other animals. Mouth parts help animals eat. How are the teeth in the pictures different? The zebra has flat teeth. The lion has pointed teeth.

How do teeth help an animal eat? A zebra is a **plant eater**. The zebra's flat teeth help it grind plants. Lions are **meat eaters**. The lion's pointed teeth can tear meat.

We have flat teeth. We also have pointed teeth. We can eat both plants and meat.

Some animals do not have teeth. They use other mouth parts to help them eat. The whale has plates called baleen. When it scoops up food, water gets into its mouth. The whale pushes the water out. The baleen stops the food from getting out, too.

▲ **gray whale**

◀ **chameleon**

The chameleon has a long tongue. It uses its tongue to catch insects. A chameleon's tongue may be longer than its body.

The hummingbird has a long beak. It has a long tongue, too. These body parts help the hummingbird get nectar from inside a flower.

Reading Check **Tell** how mouth parts help an animal use plants or animals to meet its needs.

LESSON 8

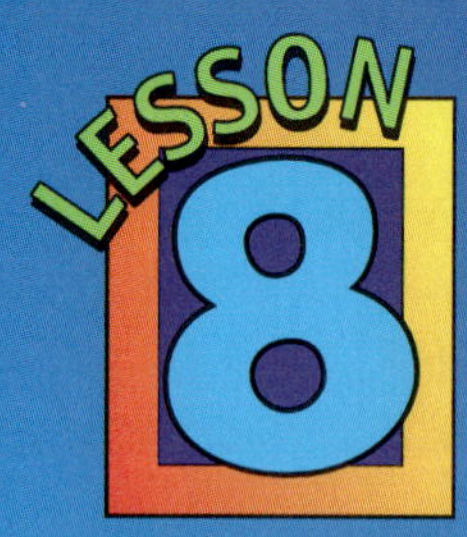

How are animals grouped?

Activity
Grouping Animals

What You Need

- discarded magazines
- Science Notebook
- scissors

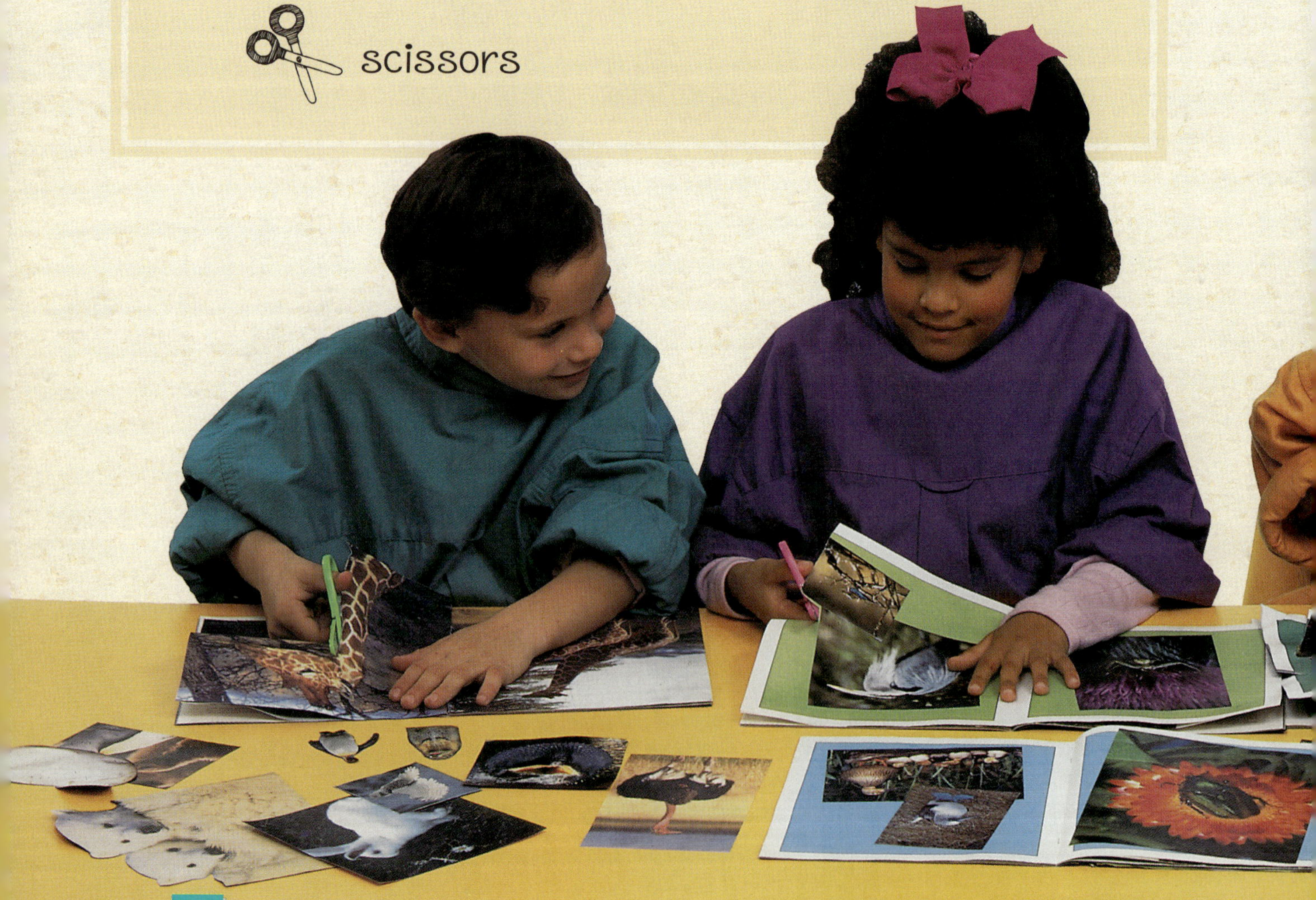

1. Cut out pictures of different kinds of animals.

2. **Sort** the animals into groups by their body covering. *Using Math*

3. **Sort** the animals into different groups. **Record** your groups.

Think! How are the animals in one group alike?

CD-ROM

Use **Science Blaster**™ **Jr.** to collect information about different plants and animals in the barnyard or in the ocean.

Many Kinds of Animals

All of these animals are mammals. Mammals are one group of animals. How are they all alike? All **mammals** have hair. They feed milk to their babies. How are the mammals in the pictures different?

Some mammals live in water. Others live on land. Some mammals swim. Others fly. Some have tusks. Other mammals have teeth. Some mammals eat meat. Others eat plants.

Different kinds of animals make other groups. What other animal groups can you think of?

◀ The macaw lives in the rain forest. It eats seeds, nuts, and berries.

The ostrich lives in grasslands. It cannot fly. It runs very fast. ▼

◀ The stingray is an ocean fish. It hides in sand.

Look at the birds and fish. All **birds** have feathers, wings, and beaks. Most can fly.

Fish live in the water. They use gills for breathing. Most fish have scales and fins.

The clown fish lives in warm water. It eats plants and fish.

The albatross lives at sea. It uses its beak to scoop up fish.

1. Make a graph like the one shown.
2. Count the number of birds and fish on these pages.
3. Color one box for each animal.

Kinds of Animals					
Birds					
Fish					
	0	1	2	3	4	5

Reading Check **Draw** a mammal, a bird, and a fish. How are they different?

How do living things grow and change?

Observing the Life Cycle of a Plant

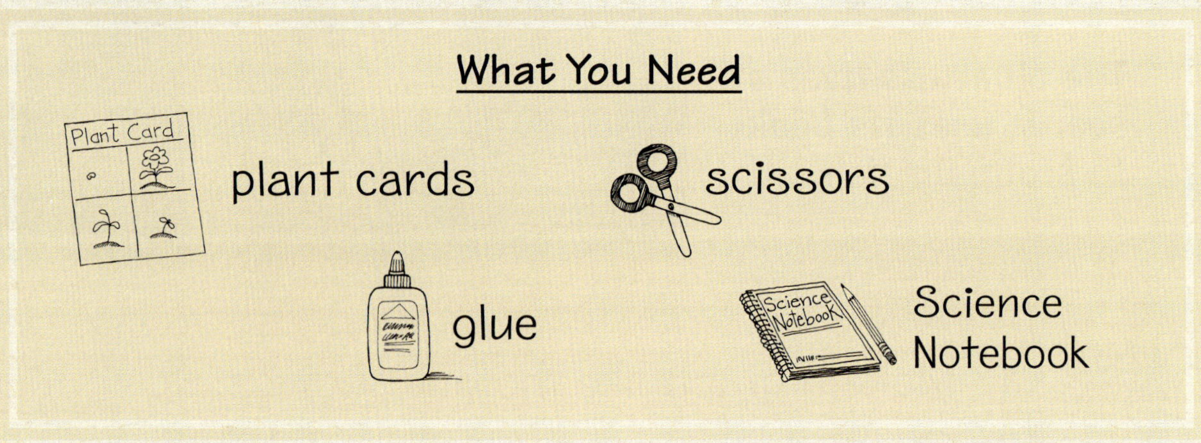

1. Cut out plant cards. Lay the cards on a table.

2. **Talk with your group** about how a plant grows.

3. **Order** the cards to show how a plant grows.

Using Math

4 Put the cards in order in your Science Notebook.

Observing the Life Cycle of a Plant	
1.	2.
3.	4.

Think! How does this plant change as it grows?

Internet Field Trip

Visit **www.eduplace.com** to observe another life cycle.

Animals Grow and Change

All animals grow and change. A **life cycle** is the order of these changes. A baby animal hatches from an egg or is born. The baby grows to be an adult. What would make the life cycle begin again?

Some animals change more than others as they grow. A caterpillar is a baby butterfly. It doesn't look like its parents at first. It changes a lot as it grows. How is this baby loon like its parents? How does it change as it grows?

Reading Check Pretend you are a baby loon. **Act out** how you grow and change.

UNIT A UNIT REVIEW

Word Power

If you need help, turn to the pages shown in blue.

Match a word with a picture. (A22–A23)

feathers hair scales

1.

2.

3.

Write the letter of the correct words.

4. A ______ feeds milk to its babies. (A40–A41)

a. insect **b.** fish **c.** bird **d.** mammal

5. An animal with pointed teeth is a ______. (A34–A35)

a. plant eater **b.** needle **c.** meat eater **d.** feather

6. A ______ has feathers, wings, and a beak. (A42–A43)

a. fish **b.** bird **c.** scale **d.** mammal

7. A place where an animal goes to be safe is a ______. (A28–A29)

a. shelter **b.** needle **c.** scale **d.** mammal

8. The order of changes from a baby to an adult is a ______. (A46–A47)

a. shell **b.** shelter **c.** scale **d.** life cycle

Using Science Ideas

How could you sort these plants into groups?

Writing in Science

Make up a new animal. Decide what your animal will look like. Use these questions to help you.

1. Will your animal fly, walk, or swim?
2. What kind of body covering will it have?
3. What kinds of mouth parts will it have?

Draw a picture of your animal. Show where it might live and what it might eat. Tell why you chose that home and food.

Classify

Look at the animals. Decide if they have feathers, scales, or hair.

Copy the word webs. Fill in the animal names next to their body coverings.

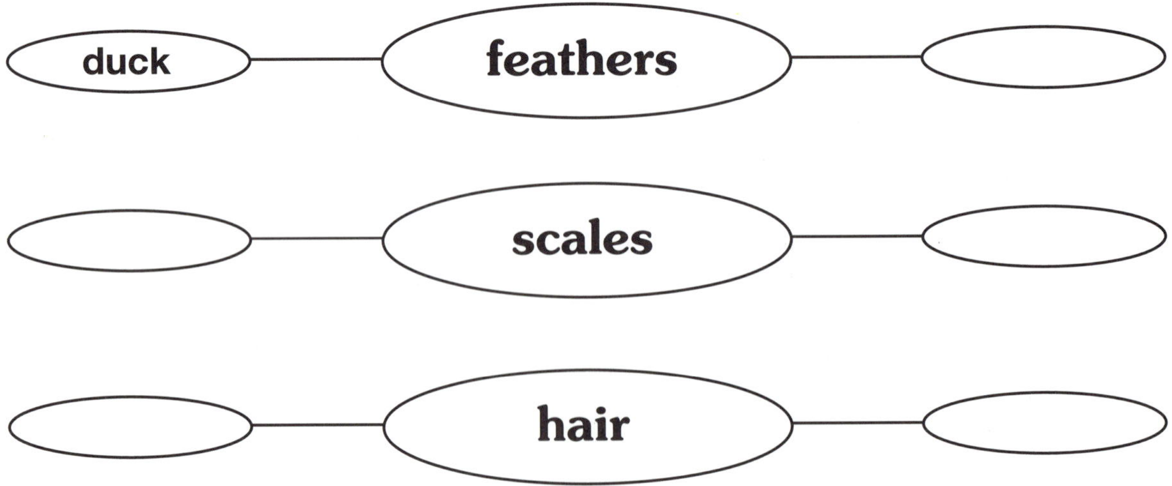

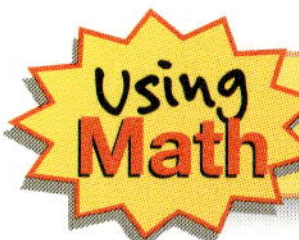

Using a Bar Graph

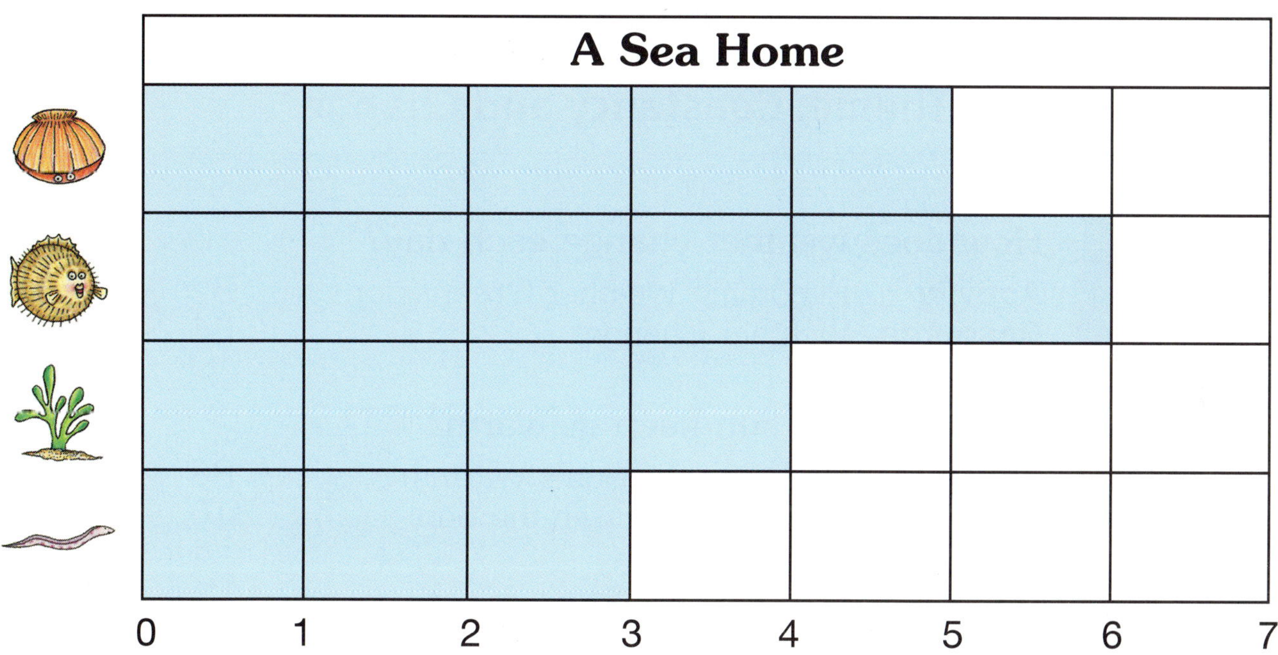

Use the graph to answer the questions.

1. How many [clam] are in this sea home?
2. How many more [puffer fish] than [plant] are there?
3. How many [worm] and [plant] are there in all?
4. Are there more [clam] or [worm] ?
5. How many living things are there in all?

Weather and Seasons

Theme: Constancy and Change

How does weather change each day?

Recording Weather Observations

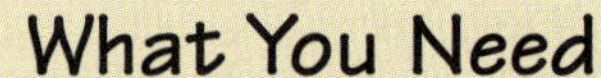

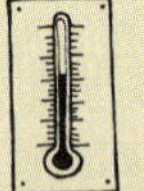 thermometer

 weather symbols

 crayons

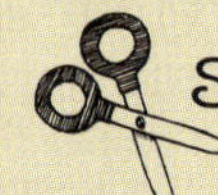 scissors

 glue

 wind profiler

Science Notebook

1. **Look at** the sky. **Record** whether it is sunny, cloudy, or foggy.

2. **Measure** and **record** the temperature.

3. Look for signs of wind blowing. **Record** what the wind is doing to leaves, flags, or trees.

4. Look for precipitation. **Record** what you see.

5. Repeat steps 1–4 each day.

Think! How did the weather change?

Find Out More!

CD-ROM

Use the **Science Blaster Jr.** weather station to observe and compare the weather around the world.

Weather Changes

Is it sunny? Is it windy? Is it raining? These are questions about the air outside or **weather**. What questions can you ask about the weather?

The weather changes every day. Look at the pictures. What was the weather each day?

On Monday it was sunny. On Tuesday it was raining. On Wednesday it was windy and sunny. What might the weather be on Thursday?

One way weather changes is that the air gets hotter or colder. The **temperature** of the air tells how hot or cold it is outside.

Monday 33°F

Tuesday 27°F

Wednesday 32°F

Thursday 40°F

Friday 45°F

Another way weather changes is that water falls from the sky. Water can fall as rain, snow, sleet, or hail. This is called precipitation.

Look at each picture. What is the weather like each day? Is it sunny or cloudy? Is it raining or snowing?

Make a chart like the one shown. Use the pictures to complete the chart.

Weather			
	Cloudy/Sunny	**Temperature**	**Rain/Snow**
Monday	cloudy	33°F	
Tuesday			

1. How many days had precipitation?
2. Were more days sunny or cloudy?
3. On what day was the temperature the highest?

Reading Check **Write** about the weather where you live. How has it changed during the past week?

How does the sun keep us warm?

Activity
Exploring the Sun's Warmth

What You Need

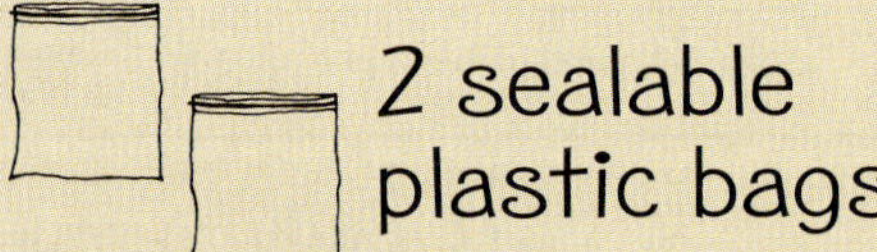

2 pieces of chocolate

2 sealable plastic bags

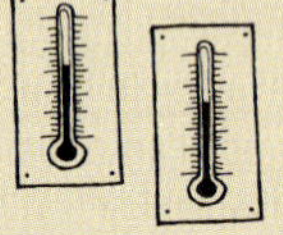

2 thermometers

Science Notebook

1. Put a piece of chocolate into each plastic bag.

2. Place one bag and a thermometer in the sun. **Record** the temperature.

3. Repeat step 2 in the shade.

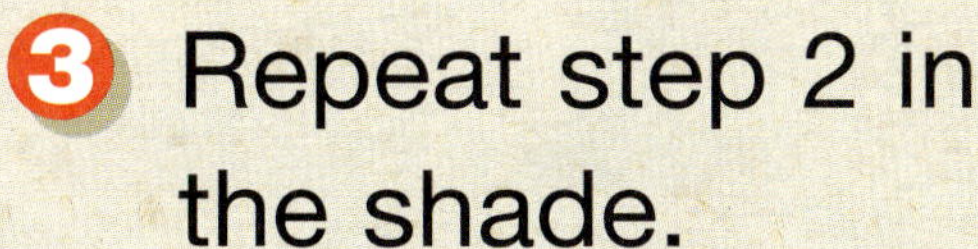

4. **Record** the temperatures in both places after 10 minutes and after 20 minutes.

5. **Look at** the chocolate in the bags. **Record** the changes.

Think! What do you think caused the changes in the chocolate?

The Warmth From the Sun

The sun heats our land. It heats our rivers and oceans, too. It even heats the air around us.

When the air is hot, we are likely to feel hot. When the air is cold, we probably feel cold. People, animals, and plants need sunlight.

In the picture, the children on the swings are in **sunlight**. The air around them is warm.

The children in the sandbox are in **shade**. A tree blocks some of the sunlight. The air around these children is a little cooler. They feel cooler.

Reading Check **Draw a picture** of a sunny area and a shady area. Where would you feel warmer?

What things get warmer?

Getting Warmer

What You Need

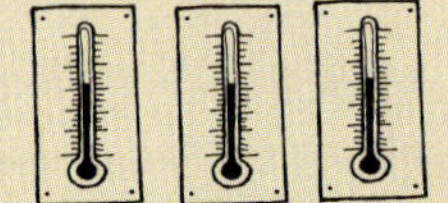 3 thermometers

 timer

Science Notebook

1. Place a thermometer on asphalt in a sunny area. Wait 3 minutes. **Record** the temperature.

2 Repeat step 1, placing the thermometer on grass.

3 Repeat step 1, placing the thermometer on concrete.

Getting Warmer	
Surface	**Temperature**
asphalt	______ °F
grass	______ °F
concrete	______ °F

4 **Compare** the temperatures in different places.

Think! Why is the temperature different in different places?

Find Out More!

Will the temperature change over the day? Wait 3 hours and repeat steps 1–4. Tell what happened.

Warm or Hot?

It is a sunny day! The sun shines on many things. It shines on bricks and water. It shines on concrete and grass. It shines on people. All these things get **heat** from the sun. Some things get warm. Others get hot.

Some things take in heat from the sun better than others. Things that take in heat better get warmer faster. Dark-colored things usually get warmer than light-colored things. Dry things usually get warmer than wet things.

Reading Check **Tell** why you might want to wear light-colored clothing on a hot day.

How does air move?

Exploring Wind

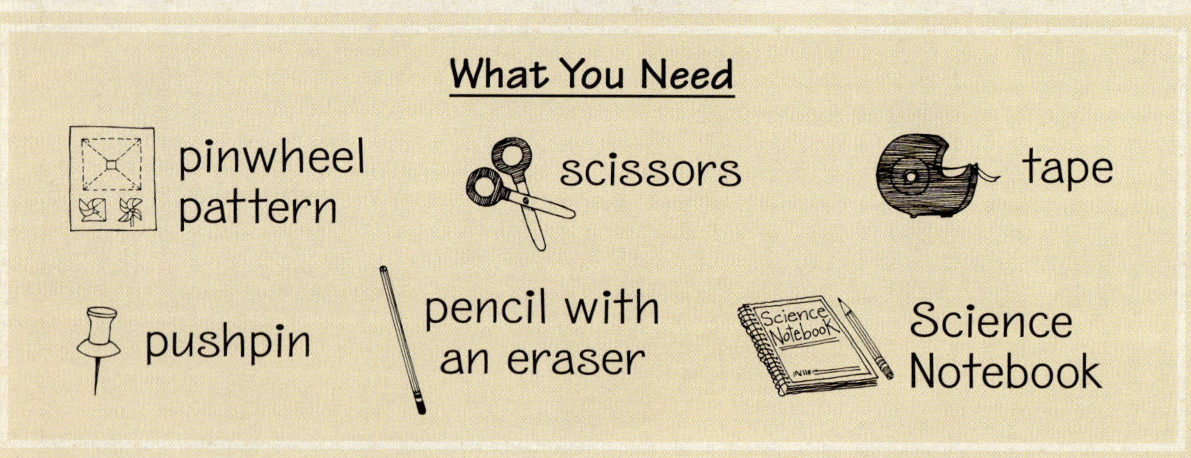

1. Cut on the dotted lines of the pinwheel pattern. Stop at the square in the center.

2 Fold the corners with dots in toward the center and tape them in place.

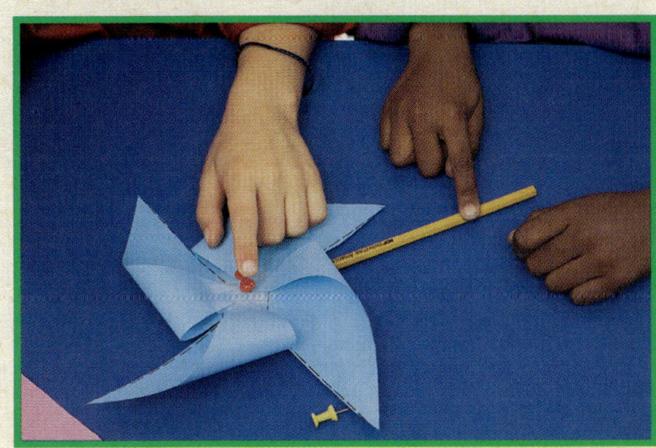

3 Put a pushpin through the center of the pinwheel and into an eraser. Be careful of the point of the pin.

4 **Test** different ways to make your pinwheel turn. **Record** what you try and what happens.

Think! What made the pinwheel turn?

Visit **www.eduplace.com** to learn more about wind.

Blowing in the Wind

Wind is moving air. Sometimes the wind moves fast. Sometimes the wind moves slowly. The wind can move many things.

The wind can make flags wave. Look at the pictures. Why do the flags look different?

In the top picture there is no wind. The air is **calm**. The flag is not waving.

In the middle picture there is a little wind. The flag waves slowly when there's a **breeze**.

In the bottom picture there is a lot of wind. Flags wave quickly in a **strong wind**.

Think of a time when you saw the wind move something. What did it move?

In autumn, wind blows the leaves. It blows the seeds in summer. Wind can blow the hat off your head and keep your kite in the sky. Wind can also move sailboats.

A sailboat will move quickly in a strong wind. In a breeze a sailboat will move slowly.

The sounds made by the wind can change. They can be very soft or very loud sounds. What sounds made by the wind have you heard?

Reading Check **Draw pictures** to show an object blowing in a strong wind and then in a breeze.

How does water change?

Examining Condensation

What You Need

2 small cans

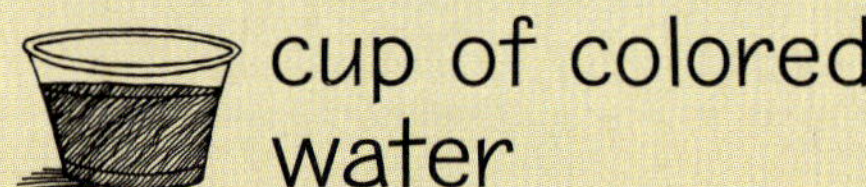
cup of colored water

cup of ice cubes

timer

Science Notebook

1. Feel the outside of an empty can. **Record** what you see and feel.

2. Put ice cubes into another can. Add some colored water.

3 Using Math Use a timer to time 5 minutes. Feel the outside of the can of ice water. **Record** what you see and feel.

Think! How are the outsides of the two cans different?

Find Out More!

Put a wet paper towel in a plastic bag and seal it. What do you think will happen? Check on it in a day. Compare your results with those of your classmates. How did the water change?

Water in the Air

The water we drink is a liquid. Water can also be a solid. **Ice** is solid water. Water can also be a gas. Water as a gas is called **water vapor**.

Look at the pictures. How did the girl make the spot on the window?

There was water vapor in the girl's breath. Her breath was warm. The window was cold. When she breathed on the window, the water vapor changed to liquid water.

Where else do you think you might find water vapor? Where do you find solid water?

High in the sky, water vapor also changes to liquid water. Tiny drops of liquid water form **clouds**. **Fog** is a cloud close to the ground. Fog and clouds are both made of tiny drops of water.

In clouds many tiny drops join to make bigger drops. These bigger drops fall as rain.

fog

If the cloud is cold enough, the water in it can fall as snow, hail, or sleet.

Sometimes water vapor near the ground cools. It forms tiny drops of water on objects. The water is called dew, or when frozen, frost.

Reading Check **Tell** about two ways that water changes.

UNIT B CHECKPOINT

Word Power

If you need help, turn to the pages shown in blue.

Match the words with a picture. (B18–B19)

breeze strong wind calm

1. 

2. 

3. 

Use these words to fill in the blanks.

clouds ice wind weather

4. The _____ tells about the air outside. (B4–B5)

5. Solid water is called _____. (B24–B25)

6. Tiny drops of liquid water form _____. (B26–B27)

7. Moving air is called _____. (B18–B19)

Solving Science Problems

You are going on a picnic. The weather is sunny. There is a breeze. The temperature is 65°F. Tell what you might wear. Decide what activities you would do. Explain your choices.

People Using Science

Meteorologist

Meteorologists study the weather. They measure and record temperature and precipitation. Looking for patterns helps them predict the weather.

Some meteorologists use computers to help predict the weather. Why is predicting the weather helpful?

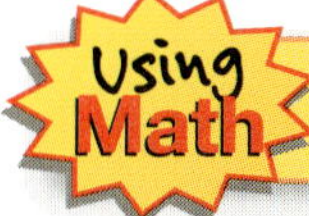

Using a Table

Abby lives in Wisconsin. In December, she recorded the amount of snow that fell each week.

December Snow				
Amount of Snow	Week 1	Week 2	Week 3	Week 4
	3 inches	8 inches	6 inches	10 inches

Use the table to answer the questions.

1. In which week did it snow the most?
2. In which week did it snow the least?
3. How much snow fell during Week 1 and during Week 3 in all?

How does the weather change with each season?

Activity

Going on a Scavenger Hunt

What You Need

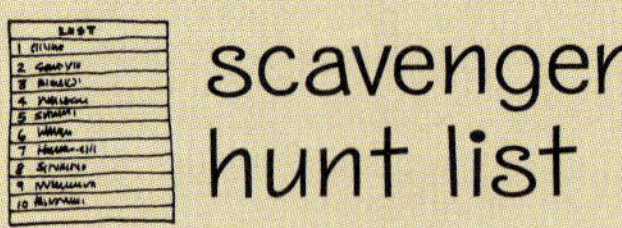
scavenger hunt list

paper bag

Science Notebook

1. Go on a scavenger hunt. **Collect** as many items from the list as you can.

2. **Talk about** items that you collected and any items that you could not find.

3. **Make a hypothesis** about how the list might be different in another season.

4. Plan a scavenger hunt list to use during another season. **Record** your list.

Think! How does the season affect what items you can find?

Find Out More!

How does the weather change over seasons? Make a plan to find out. Record the changes you observe.

Looking at Seasons

A **season** is a time of the year. The four seasons are spring, summer, autumn, and winter. The pictures show the same place in all four seasons. Weather changes from season to season. What changes do you see?

In **spring**, plants bloom and the air gets warmer. In **summer** the air gets even warmer. Then in **autumn** it gets cooler. The leaves may fall off trees. In **winter** the air gets cold. Trees may be bare. Sometimes it snows.

Reading Check **Act out** how the weather changes each season where you live.

How do people adjust to different seasons?

Activity

Cooling Off and Warming Up

What You Need

 crayons

Science Notebook

1. **Talk with your group** about ways to cool off on a hot day. **Record** your ideas.

2. **Talk with your group** about ways to warm up on a cold day. **Record** your ideas.

3. Take turns **acting out** your ideas about cooling off and warming up. Have other groups try to **guess** what you are acting out.

Think! How do people cool off and warm up? Explain how you made your decisions.

People and Seasons

What fun it is to play outside! You can have fun in all four seasons.

One picture shows a summer activity. The other picture shows a winter activity. How can you tell what the weather is like in each picture?

People change what they do and wear as the seasons change. In the hot summer, people wear less clothing. Some people swim to cool off. When it is cold in winter, people wear more clothing.

Reading Check **List** things that people do when the weather is hot and when it is cold.

How do animals change when the seasons change?

Keeping Warm

What You Need

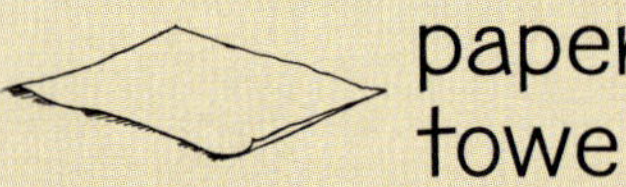
paper towel

fiberfill

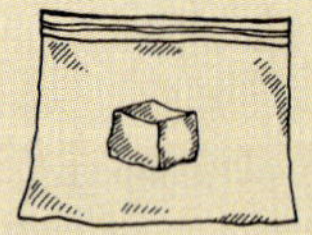
ice cube in a sealable plastic bag

Science Notebook

1. Pretend a paper towel on your arm is an animal's thin summer coat. Put an ice cube on the paper towel for about 1 minute. **Record** how it feels.

2 Pretend some fiberfill is an animal's thick winter coat. Put it between the paper towel and your arm.

3 Hold the ice cube on top of the thick winter coat for about 1 minute. **Record** how it feels. **Compare** your results.

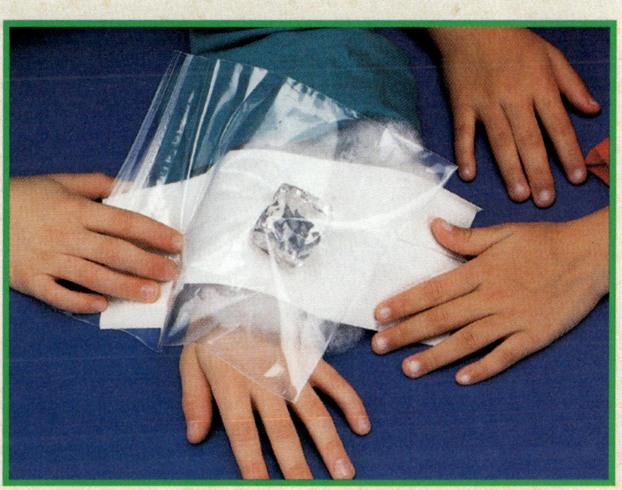

Think! How does a thick winter coat help an animal?

Internet Field Trip

Visit **www.eduplace.com** to learn about animals and seasons.

Animals and Seasons

Animals also change with the seasons. The first picture shows a weasel in summer. It has brown fur in summer. The weasel lives in the forest. The brown fur helps the weasel hide from other animals.

The second picture shows a weasel in winter. Some weasels live in cold places. Each winter they grow a coat of white fur. This color helps a weasel hide in the snow.

In the spring the weasel sheds its white fur, and a new coat of brown fur grows.

Canada geese

ground squirrels

Animals get ready for winter in other ways. Winter in many places is too cold for some birds. They do not have enough food to eat. These birds migrate. Geese **migrate** by flying to the same warm place every winter. In the spring they return to the place where they started.

American bison

Some animals, like the ground squirrel, **hibernate**. They sleep most of the winter. Their bodies slow down, so they don't need much food.

Other animals grow thick winter coats. The bison's coat keeps it warm in the cold weather.

Reading Check Choose an animal. **Tell** how the animal gets ready for winter.

How do plants change in different seasons?

Watching Seeds Grow

1 Put soil in egg cartons. Plant a radish seed in each egg cup.

2. Water all seeds the same amount. Do not overwater.

3. Keep one carton in a refrigerator. Keep the other carton in a warm place. Water the seeds every day.

4. **Compare** the two containers of seeds. **Record** what you see.

Think! How does temperature affect how seeds grow?

Plants and Seasons

Plants also change with the seasons. The pictures show an oak tree in each of the four seasons. The large picture is autumn. How can you tell? The leaves have changed color. What seasons are shown in the other pictures?

The top picture is winter. The air is colder. The leaves have fallen from the tree. The next picture is spring. The air has gotten warmer. There are buds on the tree. The bottom picture is summer. There are many green leaves.

Reading Check **Write** about what the tree will look like next. How do you know what will happen?

UNIT B

UNIT REVIEW

Word Power

If you need help, turn to the pages shown in blue.

Match a word with a picture. (B32–B33)

winter autumn summer

1. 

2. 

3. 

Write the letter of the correct word.

4. Birds ______ to warmer places in winter. (B42–B43)

a. weather **b.** migrate **c.** season **d.** hibernate

5. Ground squirrels ______ for the winter. (B42–B43)

a. migrate **b.** season **c.** hibernate **d.** clouds

6. ______ from the sun warms the earth. (B14–B15)

a. Shade **b.** Heat **c.** Fog **d.** Season

7. When water is a gas, it is called ______. (B24–B25)

a. wind **b.** shade **c.** season **d.** water vapor

8. The ______ of the air tells how hot or cold it is. (B4–B5)

a. fog **b.** clouds **c.** rain **d.** temperature

Using Science Ideas

What season is shown? How can you tell?

Writing in Science

Make a chart like the one shown. Fill in what plants look like in each season. Then list what people wear or do in each season. Tell why.

Season	Plants	People
spring		
summer		
autumn		
winter		

Compare and Contrast

The pictures below show how Anita's yard looks in two different seasons. Some things are the same in each season. Some things are different.

Use the pictures to answer the questions.

1. Draw or list the things that are the same in each season.
2. Draw or list things that you see only in the winter season.
3. Tell which things change from season to season.

Using MATH SKILLS

Using Math Measure

Jason got a new weather kit. He likes to use the rain gauge to measure the rainfall. He measured the rain on four different days.

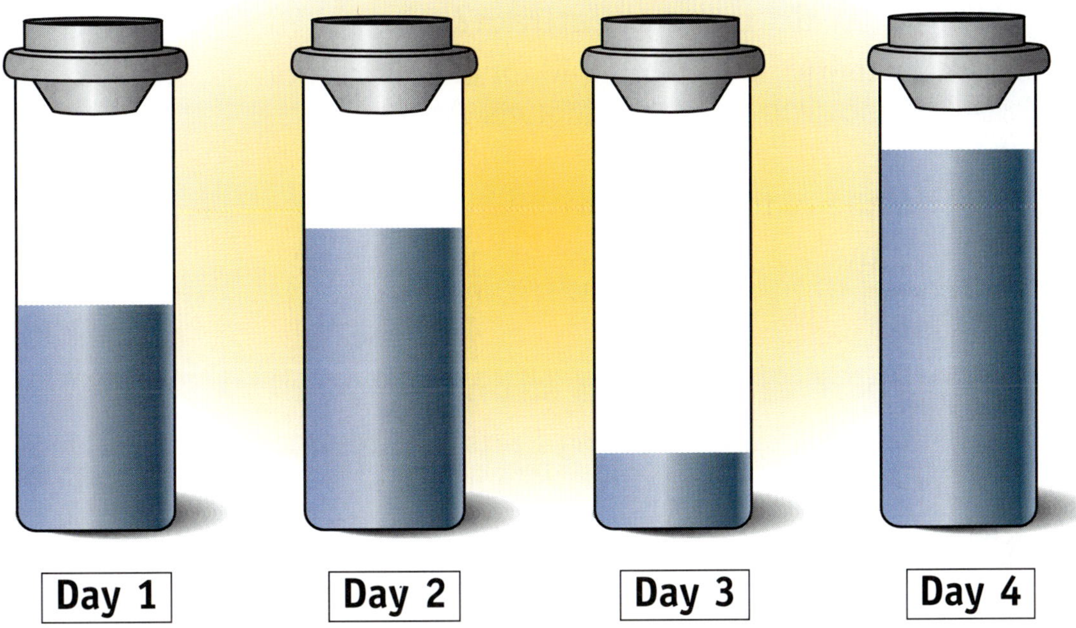

1. About how much rain is in each gauge? Record your guess in a chart like the one below.

2. Next, use a centimeter ruler to measure the rainfall in each gauge. Record the measure.

Measuring Rain		
	Guess	Measure
Day 1	___ cm	___ cm

Magnets

Themes: Systems; Scale

N
S

S
N

N
S

S
N

What do magnets attract?

Exploring Magnetic Attraction

What You Need

bag of objects

magnet

Science Notebook

1 **Predict** whether a magnet will attract each object. **Record** your predictions.

Exploring Magnetic Attraction		
Object	Prediction	Result

2 **Test** the objects and **record** your results. **Sort** the objects.

3 **Compare** your results with your predictions. **Talk about** which results surprised you.

Think! What did you find out about the objects that magnets attract?

Find Out More!

What other things in your classroom are attracted by a magnet? Make a plan to find out. Share your results.

Things Magnets Attract

A magnet is a piece of metal. It can pull some things toward itself and hold them. The magnet **attracts** these things. Look at the picture. Which things might a magnet attract? A **magnet** attracts things made of iron, steel, and nickel.

Magnets do not attract all things. A magnet will not pick up paper or plastic. It will not pick up most soda pop cans. These things are not made of iron, steel, or nickel. What things in the picture will a magnet not attract?

Reading Check **Write** about something that a magnet attracts. What is it made of?

What is magnetic force?

Activity
Discovering Magnetic Force

What You Need

2 pieces of tape
magnet
objects to test
paper clip tied to a piece of yarn
Science Notebook

1. Tape the ends of a piece of yarn to a table.

2. Touch a magnet to the paper clip. Use the magnet to make the paper clip stand up.

3. Slowly pull the magnet up so that it's not touching the paper clip.

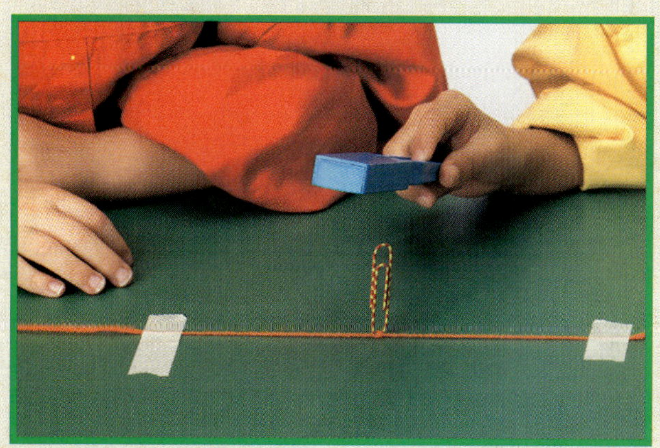

4. **Test** different objects by placing them between the clip and the magnet. **Record** what happens.

Think! Which objects made the clip fall? How are they alike?

Internet Field Trip

Visit **www.eduplace.com** to learn more about magnetic force.

Force of Magnets

Sometimes a magnet can attract things without touching them. A magnet has a force around it. **Magnetic force** attracts things made of some kinds of metal to the magnet. This force can go through the air.

▲ The magnets attract the paper clips. When the magnets are moved, the trucks also move.

Look at the pictures. How are the children making the trucks move? The trucks have paper clips on them. The magnets and the clips are not touching. The magnetic force from the magnets goes through the air to the paper clips. This makes the trucks move.

Magnetic force goes through air. It also goes through some objects.

▲ Magnetic force goes through the paper to the refrigerator. All of these magnets can hold up one picture.

▲ Some magnets are weaker than others. Their force can only go through thin objects.

Some magnets are very strong. Their force can go through thick objects. ▼

Use the table to answer the questions.

Magnet	How many it holds
● (blue circle)	1 picture
■ (red square)	5 pictures
▲ (yellow triangle)	10 pictures

1. Which magnet can hold 10 pictures?
2. Which magnet is the weakest?
3. How many more pictures can the ▲ hold than the ■ ?

Reading Check **Act out** how it would feel to be a paper clip being pulled by a magnet.

Where are magnets strongest?

Activity

Comparing Parts of a Magnet

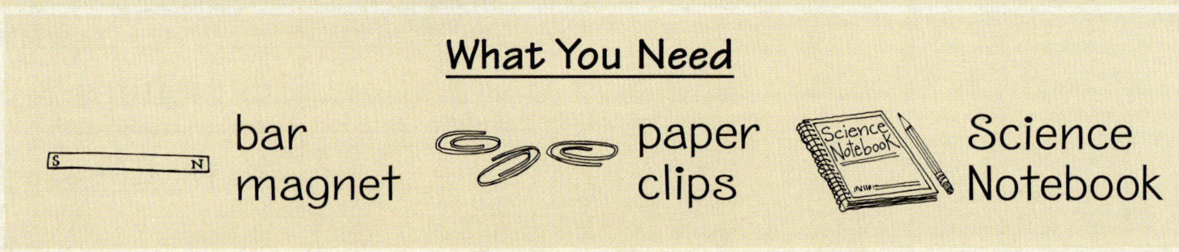

1. Hold up a bar magnet and make a paper clip chain at one end. Count the paper clips. **Record** the number.

2. Remove the clips. Make a new chain in the middle of the magnet. Count the clips. **Record** the number.

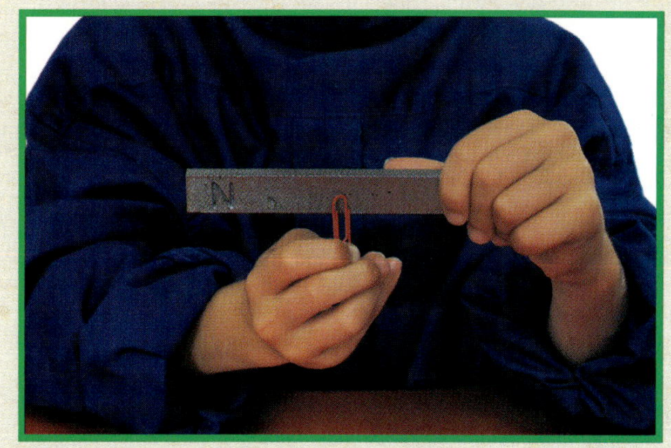

3. Remove the clips and make a chain at the other end of the magnet. Count the clips. **Record** the number.

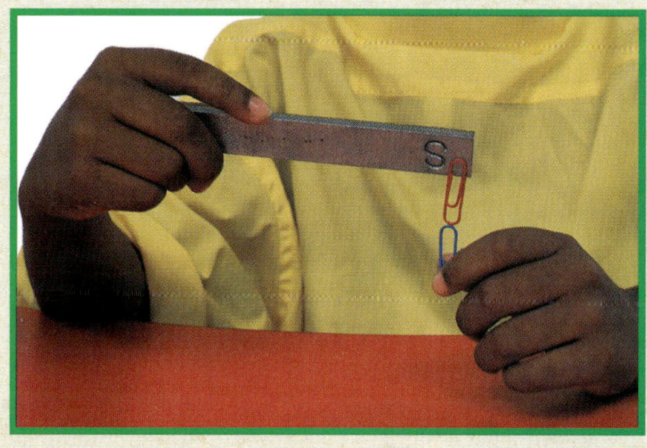

4. Using Math **Make a bar graph** to show the number of clips in each chain. **Compare** the numbers.

Clips on the Magnet

	N	Middle	S
6			
5			
4			
3			
2			
1			
0			

Think! **What does your bar graph tell you about the strength of different parts of your bar magnet?**

Strength of Magnets

Some magnets are stronger than others. Some strong magnets can pick up a car.

Look at the picture. Which magnet is the largest? The **bar magnet** is one of the largest. It is the long, straight silver magnet.

The gray circle or **ring magnet** is one of the smallest magnets. Which magnet do you think can pick up the most paper clips?

You might think a large magnet can pick up more clips than a small magnet. Turn the page to find out which magnet is strongest.

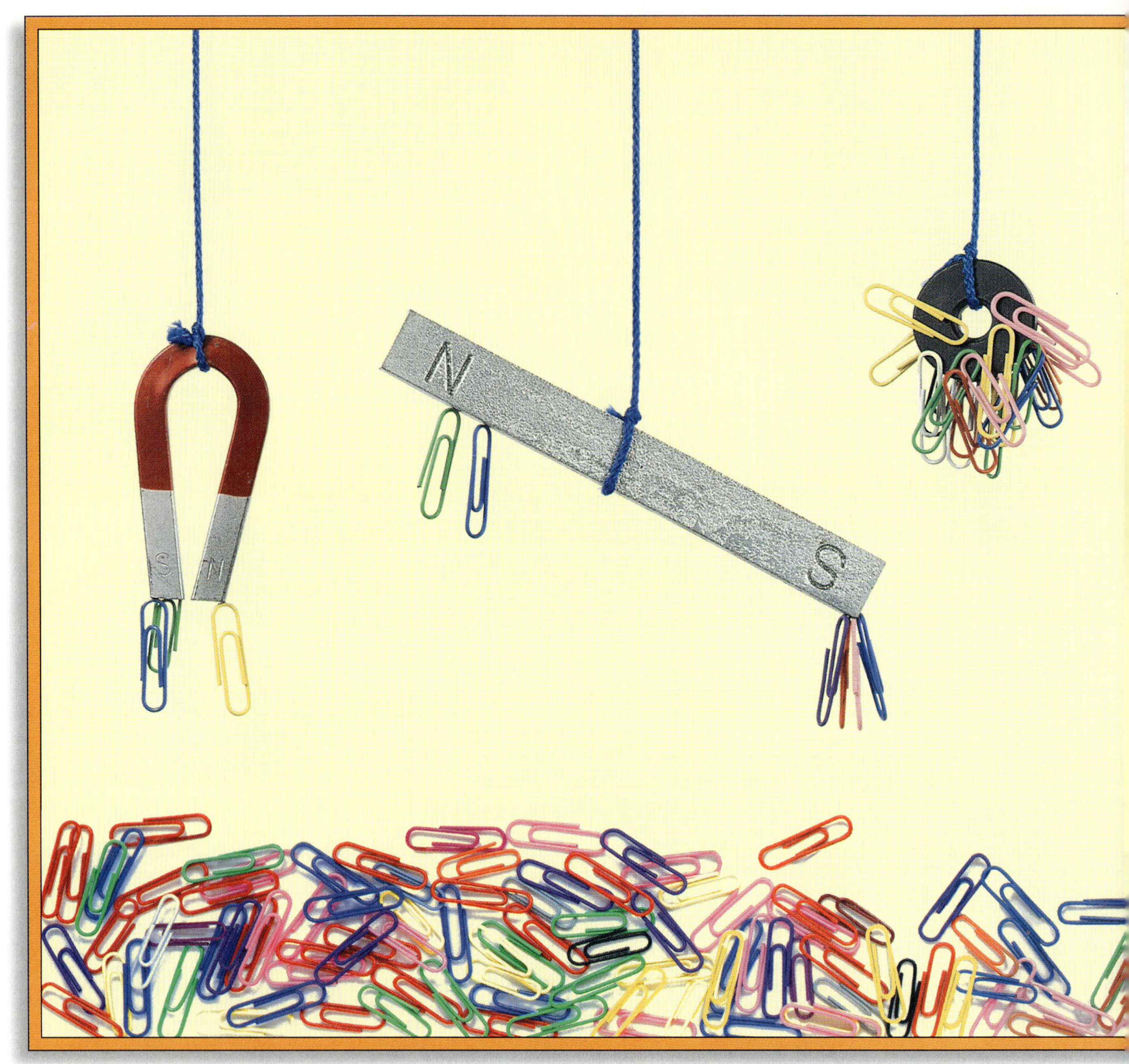

Each magnet picked up some clips. The picture helps you compare the strength of the magnets. A small magnet can be strong. A large magnet can be weak. The bar magnet picked up just six paper clips. The ring magnet picked up many more paper clips.

Find the places on each magnet where you see the clips. The clips are near the poles. Magnets are strongest at their **poles**. Poles are in different places on different magnets. They might be on the ends or on the sides.

Reading Check **Draw a picture** of two kinds of magnets. Show where each one is strongest.

UNIT C

CHECKPOINT

Word Power

If you need help, turn to the pages shown in blue.

Match the words with a picture. (C14–C15)

bar magnet   ring magnet

1. 

2. 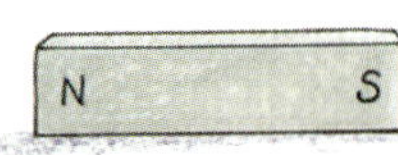

Use these words to fill in the blanks.

attract   magnet   magnetic force

3. _____ goes through the air and some things. (C8–C9)

4. A _____ attracts things made of iron, steel, and nickel. (C4–C5)

5. Some magnets _____ things and hold them. (C4–C5)

Solving Science Problems

Randy and Tara were playing. Randy said that he could make his toy bus move without touching it. Tell how he could do this.

People Using Science

Crane Operator

A crane operator sometimes uses a special magnet on the crane to lift steel and some other metals. The magnet attracts and holds large pieces of metals.

The electromagnet lifts the metals above large bins. The operator then turns off the magnet and the metal falls into the bin. Why do you think this kind of magnet is useful?

Using Math Data From a Picture

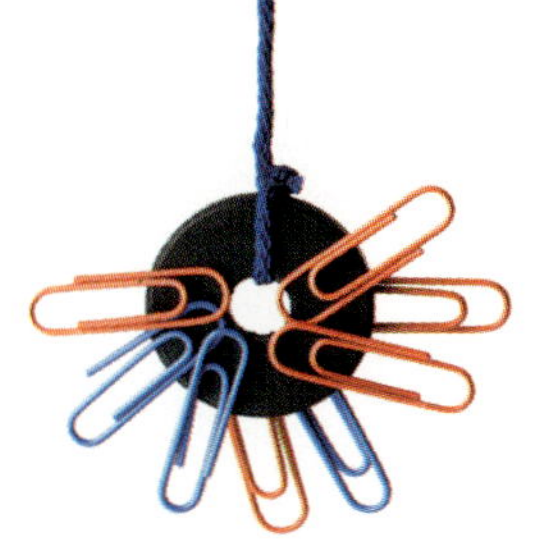

Look at the picture. Write a number sentence to answer each question. Then solve.

1. How many orange and blue paper clips are there in all?
2. How many more green paper clips are there than yellow paper clips?

What do the poles of a magnet do?

Activity

Observing the Poles of Magnets

What You Need

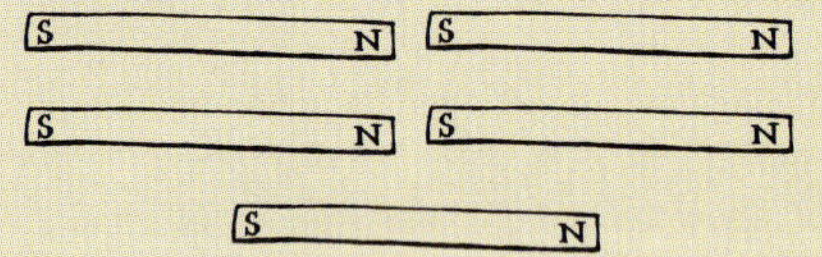

5 bar magnets

Science Notebook

1. Place two magnets end to end and **record** what happens.
2. Turn one of the magnets around and **record** what happens.

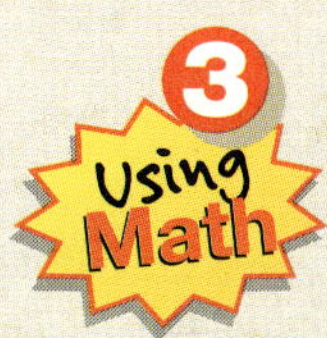

3 Using Math Place five magnets end to end so that they stick together. **Draw** the line of magnets and label the poles.

Think! How can you line up bar magnets so that they push or pull on each other?

Find Out More!

How are the poles of other magnets like the poles of bar magnets? Ask questions. Make a plan to find answers. Share your results with your classmates.

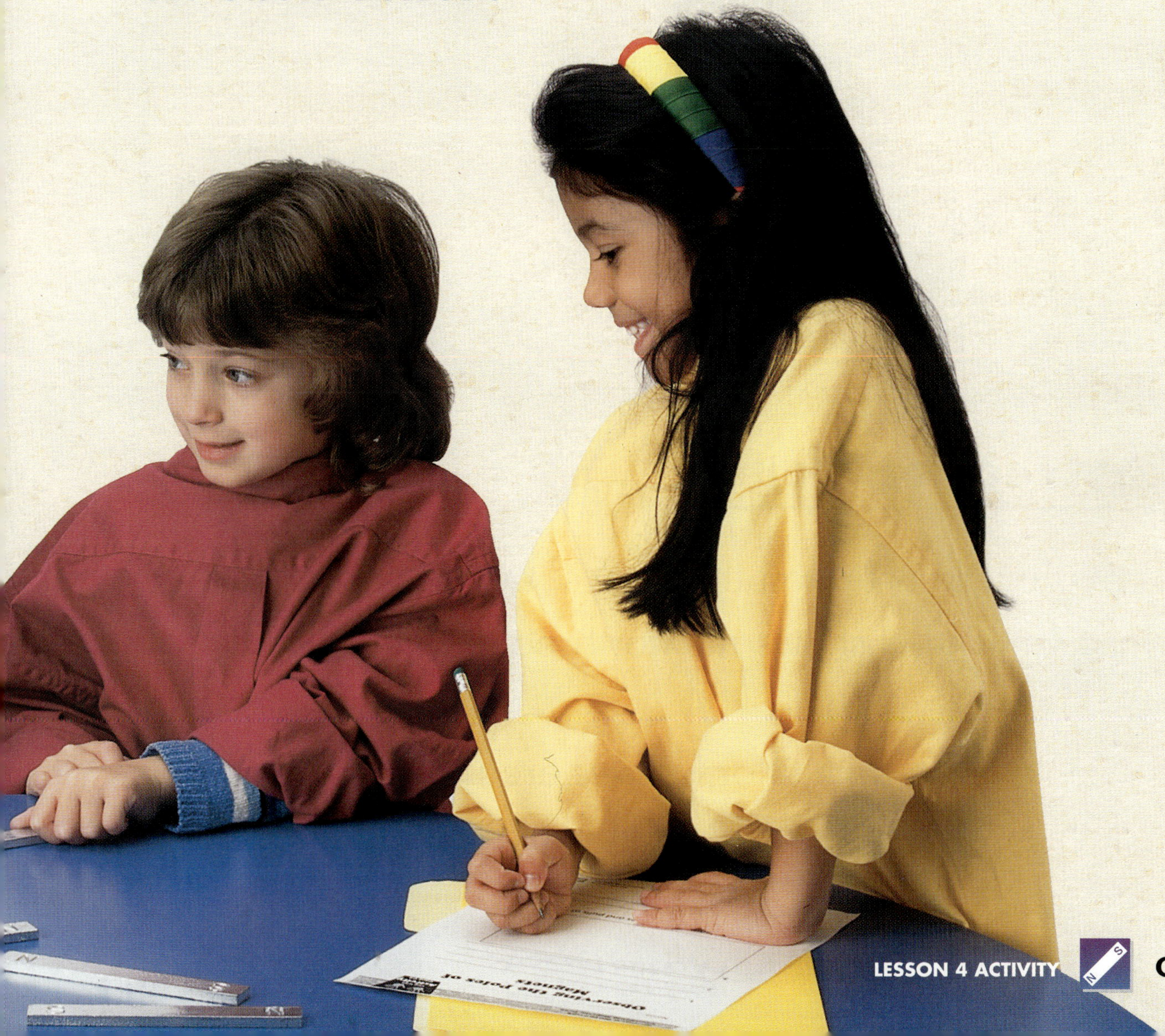

Attract or Repel?

Bar magnets are on these toys. Look at one magnet. The N shows the north pole. The S shows the south pole.

Look at the train. North poles are next to south poles. **Unlike poles** attract each other.

Look at the boats. North poles are next to north poles. South poles are next to south poles. **Like poles** push away from each other. Like poles **repel** each other. How could you get the boats to connect? Turn some boats so that unlike poles are next to each other.

Look at the photos of the ring magnets. The poles are not marked with N or S. How can you tell if like poles or unlike poles are next to each other? In the first stack, the magnets attract each other. These magnets have unlike poles next to each other.

In the second stack, the magnets seem to be floating. These magnets have like poles next to each other. The magnets repel each other.

Look at the two stacks of magnets below. Are the poles next to each other like or unlike?

Reading Check **Tell** what happens if you put the like poles of two magnets together.

What is a magnetic field?

Activity

Making Magnetic Patterns

What You Need

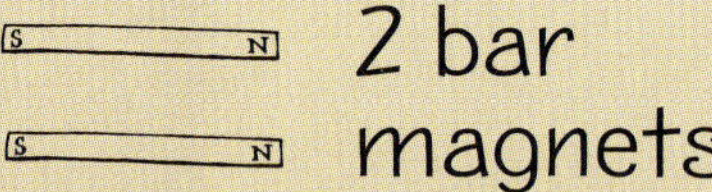

2 bar magnets

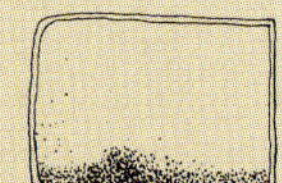

plastic sheet with iron filings

Science Notebook

1. Shake the plastic sheet to spread the iron filings out. **Draw** what you see.

2. Lay two magnets on the sheet end to end. Put two unlike poles next to each other but not touching. **Draw** what you see.

3. Shake the plastic sheet. Then place the magnets so that like poles are next to each other but not touching. **Draw** what you see.

Think! How are your three drawings different? Tell why.

Find Out More!

Use different kinds of magnets. Look for the pattern that the iron filings make around the magnets. Then sort the magnets by the patterns made by the filings.

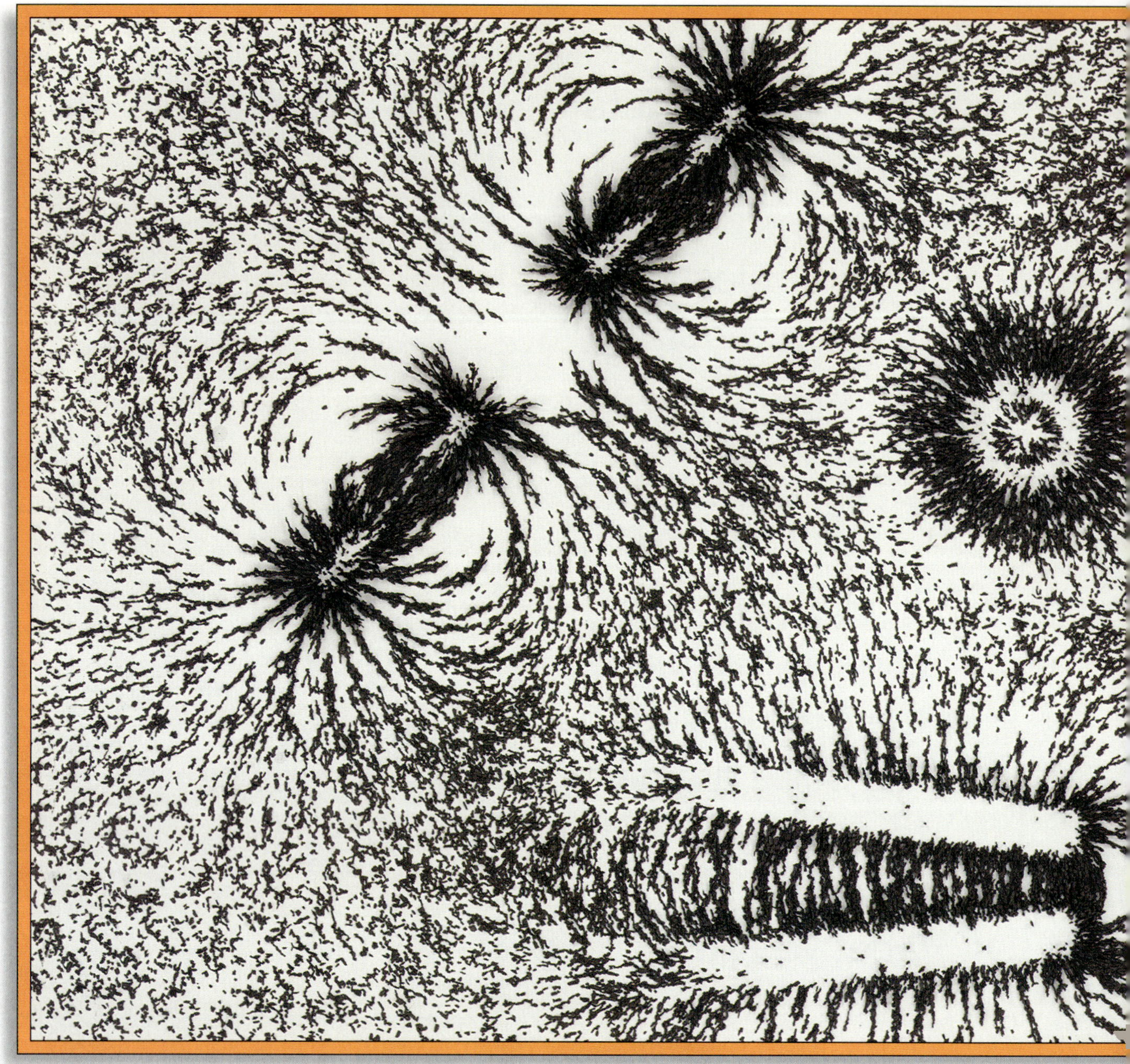

What's Around a Magnet?

Each magnet can make its own pattern. Look at the patterns. They are made of iron filings.

The patterns show the magnetic field of each magnet. A **magnetic field** is all around a magnet. It's where a magnet's force works.

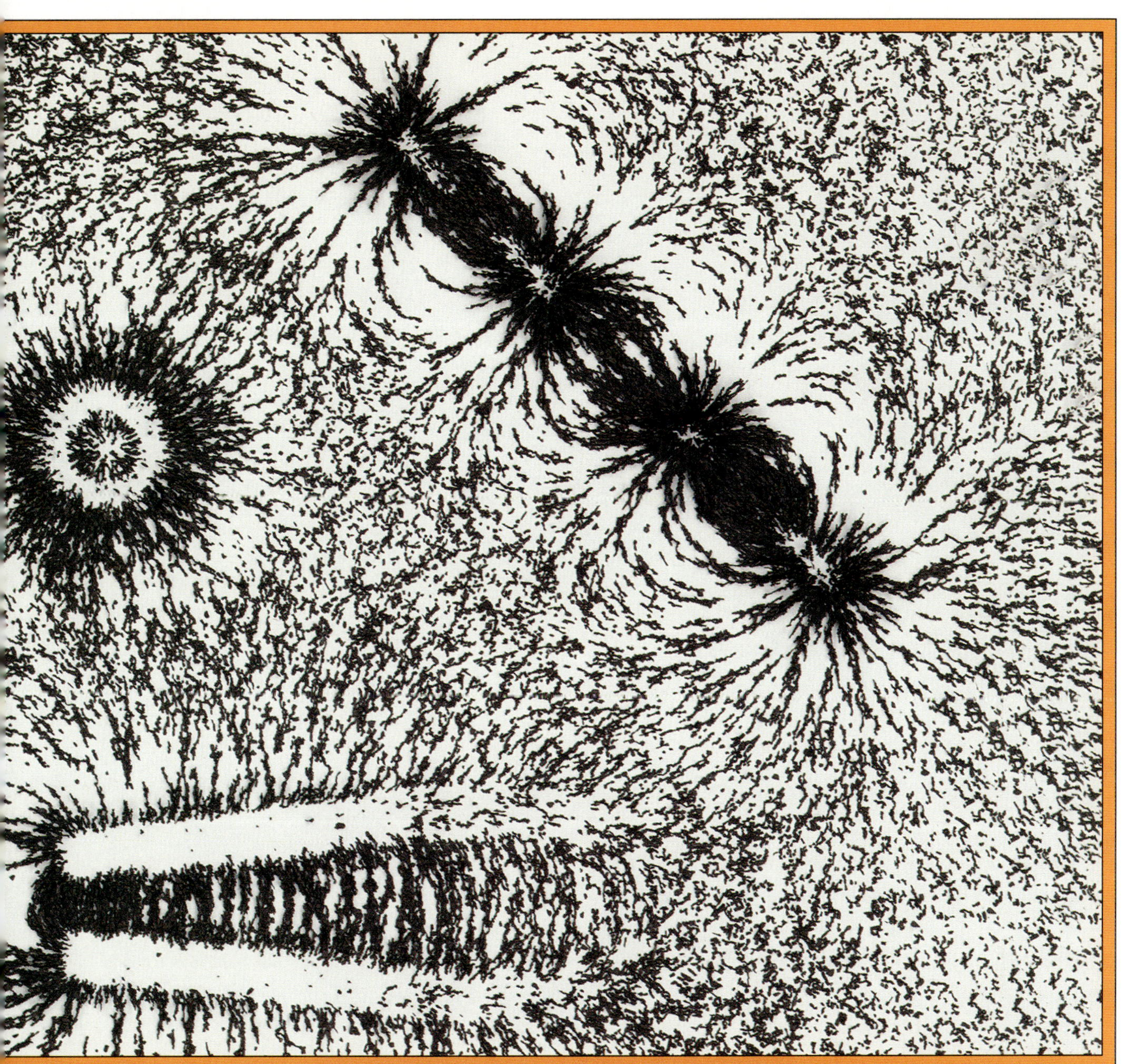

Look for places where there are the most iron filings. That's where the force is strongest.

Now look for places where there are few iron filings. That's where the force is weakest. What magnets made these patterns? Turn the page to find out.

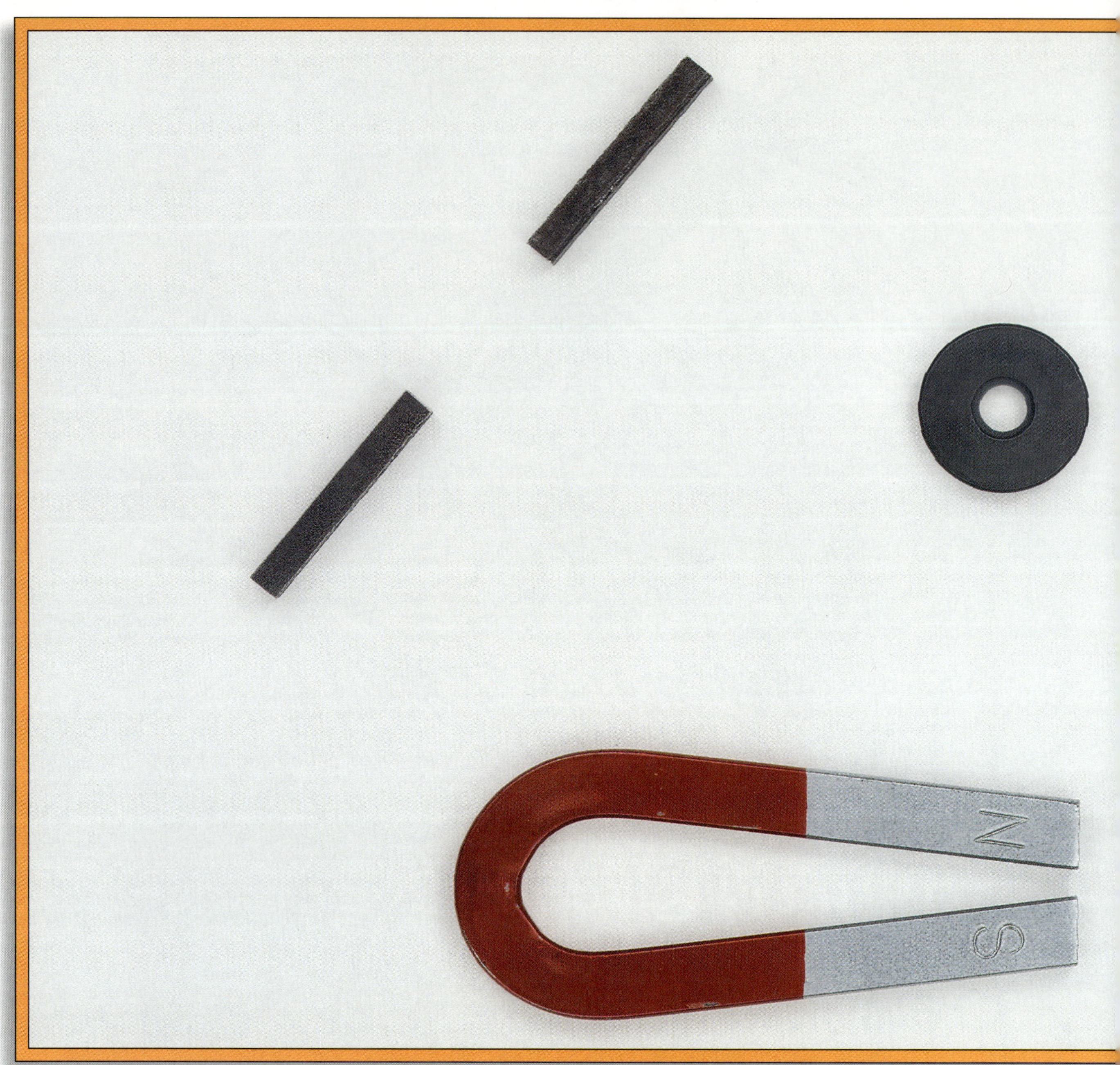

Think about the picture you just saw. It was made with these magnets.

A sheet of paper was put on top of the magnets. Iron filings were sprinkled on the paper. The filings made patterns. The patterns show the magnetic fields.

Look at the red magnets. Unlike poles are facing each other. Look back at the pattern they made with iron filings. The unlike poles attract each other and the filings. Which magnets have like poles facing each other?

Reading Check **Draw a picture** to show a pattern made by two magnets and some iron filings.

What is a temporary magnet?

Activity

Making Magnets

1. Touch a spoon to some paper clips. Lift the spoon and **draw** what you see.

2 Use a magnet to stroke the spoon twenty times in one direction.

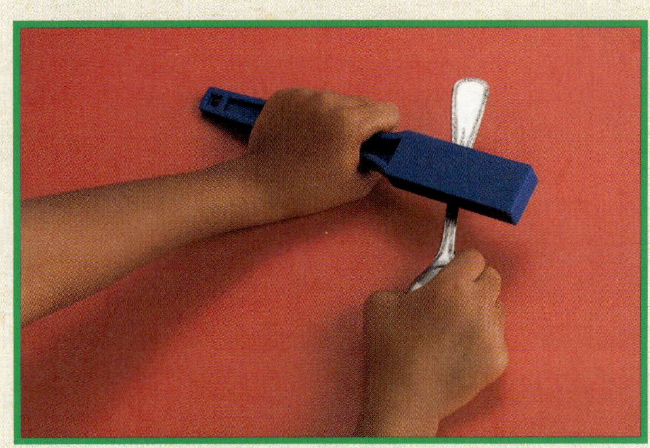

3 Touch the spoon to the paper clips again. Lift the spoon. **Draw** what you see.

Think! Compare your drawings. What happened to the spoon?

Find Out More!

Do you think your spoon magnet is as strong as other magnets? Ask questions. Make a plan to find answers. Share your results.

Making a Magnet

Look at the picture story. The girl wants to fish, too. She makes a magnet. A **temporary magnet** won't last long. The girl strokes a steel key with the boy's magnet. She strokes the key many times in the same direction.

Think of things that a magnet attracts. You can use any of those things to make a temporary magnet. What can you use? You can use an iron nail or a steel spoon. Why can't you use a plastic jar to make a magnet?

Reading Check **Write** directions to tell someone how to make and use a temporary magnet.

LESSON 7

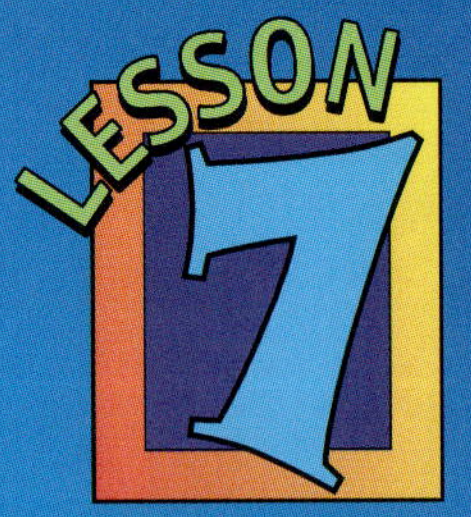

How are a compass and a magnet alike?

Activity

Using a Magnet as a Compass

What You Need

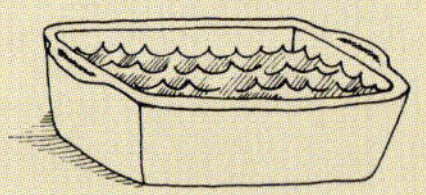
pan of water

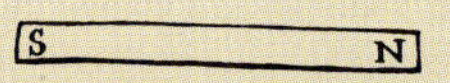

bar magnet

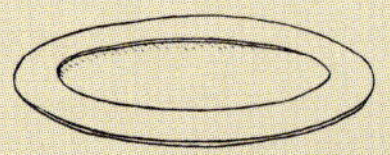
plate

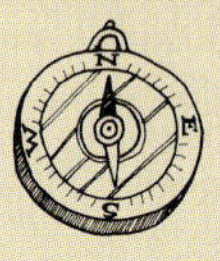
magnetic compass

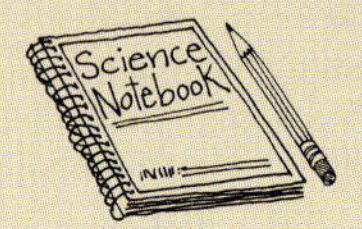

Science Notebook

1. Float a plate in a pan of water.

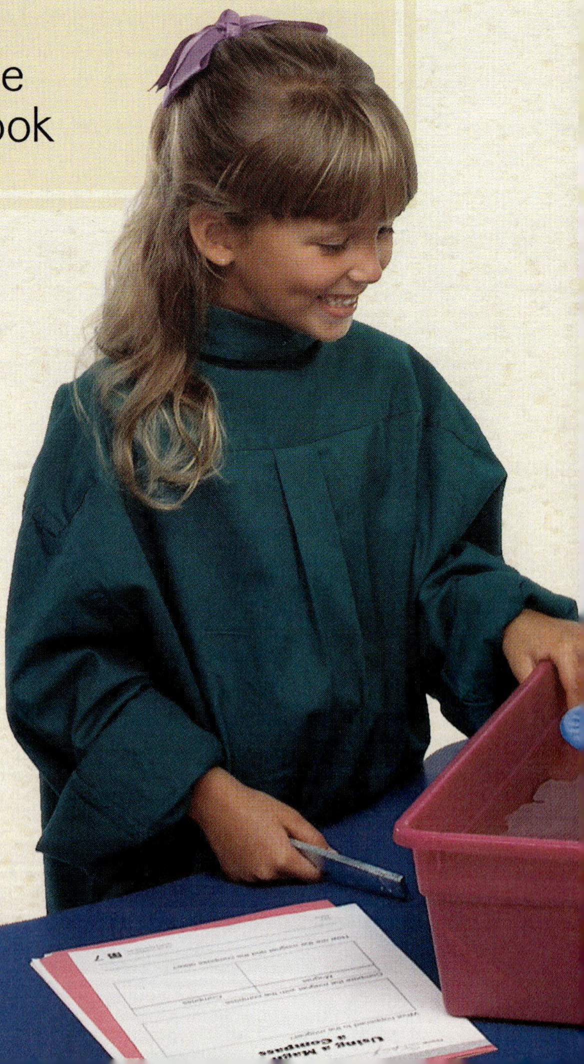

2 Put a bar magnet in the center of the plate. **Record** what happens.

3 **Compare** the poles of the magnet with the needle on a compass. **Record** what you see.

Think! **How are the poles of the magnet and the compass needle alike?**

Internet Field Trip

Visit **www.eduplace.com** to find out more about the earth's magnetic field.

Finding Your Way

The earth is like a bar magnet. It has a north pole. It also has a south pole.

A compass needle is a bar magnet. It has a north-seeking pole. This pole points to the place where the earth's north pole is.

The people in these photos are using compasses. A **compass** is a tool. It is used to show direction. The hikers turn the compass until the needle points to the N. This tells them which way is north.

Reading Check **Tell** a story about using a bar magnet to find your way home.

UNIT C UNIT REVIEW

Word Power

If you need help, turn to the pages shown in blue.

Match the words with a picture. (C14, C34, C39)

bar magnet   compass   temporary magnet

1.

2.

3.

Use these words to fill in the blanks.

4. A magnet is strongest at its ______. (C16–C17)

a. south **b.** attract **c.** poles **d.** compass

5. When the poles of two magnets pull toward each other, they are ______ poles. (C22–C23)

a. like **b.** unlike **c.** south **d.** magnetic

6. The north poles of two magnets push away, or ______ each other. (C22–C23)

a. repel **b.** attract **c.** poles **d.** bar magnet

7. When the poles of two magnets push away from each other, they are ______ poles. (C22–C23)

a. north **b.** like **c.** unlike **d.** magnets

8. The area around a magnet where the force is felt is the ______. (C28–C29)

a. repel **b.** attract **c.** poles **d.** magnetic field

Using Science Ideas

a. Which things shown will a magnet attract? List or draw them.

b. Which things shown will a magnet not attract? List or draw them.

c. Explain how you decided which things a magnet would attract.

Writing in Science

What things do you think a magnet will attract through? Talk about the problem you are trying to solve and some of your solutions. Explain how you would test your ideas. Record your results, and share them with your classmates.

Using Reading Skills

Predicting Outcomes

Look at each row of magnets. Predict what will happen if you push the magnet on the right side in each row toward the other magnets.

Write or draw your predictions. Use magnets to test your predictions. Then draw pictures to show what happened.

1. S N | S N   S N

2. S N   N S   S N

3. S N | S N   N S

4. S N   N S   N S

Tell how your predictions matched your results.

Using Math Skills

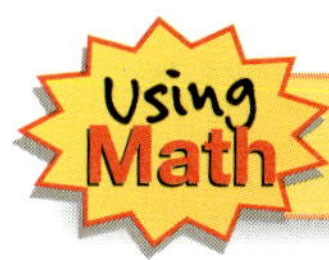

Making a Table

Susana and Abdul were helping in the school store. Someone dropped a box of paper clips. Susana and Abdul used these magnets to pick up the paper clips.

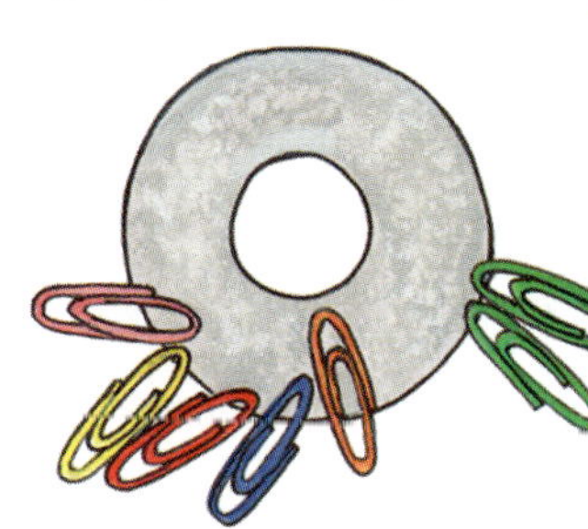

Make a table like the one below. Use the picture to complete the table.

Picking Up Paper Clips	
Type of magnet	**Number of paper clips**
N S	

Use the table to answer the questions.

1. How many paper clips did the three magnets attract altogether?

2. Which magnet would you use to pick up a box of paper clips? Tell why.

Earth's Land and Water

Themes: Systems; Models

What kinds of soil cover the earth's land?

Examining Kinds of Soil

1 **Look at** and touch three kinds of soil.

2 **Look at** each kind of soil with a hand lens.

3 **Record** what you see.

Think! How are these kinds of soil alike, and how are they different?

Looking at Soil

Soil covers much of the earth's land. Look at the layers of soil in the picture. You see grass, a tree, and flowers growing in the soil. That's what you see when you look at the ground. You don't see the other layers.

The top part of soil is called **topsoil**. Roots grow down in the topsoil.

Clay soil is often under the topsoil. Big rocks are under the clay soil. The tree's roots grow down to the rocks.

Reading Check **Write** about the kinds of soil that cover the earth. What grows in soil?

What kinds of things does soil contain?

Analyzing Soil

What You Need

goggles

cup of soil

hand lens

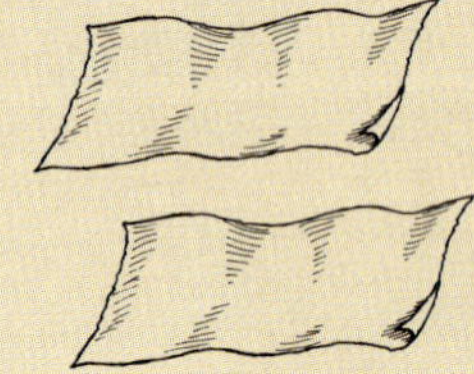
2 large sheets of paper

Science Notebook

1. Spread out soil on a sheet of paper. Use a hand lens to **look at** the soil.

2. Place things you find in the soil on another sheet of paper.

3. **Group** things that are alike. **Draw** each group.

Using Math

Think! What kinds of things did you find in the soil?

Looking Closer at Soil

Soil is made of many things. The things in the picture can become part of soil. The logs and the leaves in the picture are **once-living things**. They are not living now. When they were living, they were part of a tree.

A tree is a living thing. **Living things** need air, water, and food to stay alive.

A rock is a nonliving thing. **Nonliving things** do not need air, water, and food. What kinds of things might you find under the log? Turn the page to find out.

The log has been rolled away. What living things do you see? You see bugs and plants that live in soil. The hand lenses make them look a lot bigger than they are.

What nonliving things do you see? You see pieces of rock.

Look through the hand lenses again. What once-living things do you see? You see pieces of dry leaves and twigs. These things were once part of a tree. They no longer need air, water, and food.

Reading Check **Draw a picture** of some things you might find in soil.

What happens to soil when water is added?

Examining Soil and Water

1. Place paper towels under two paper cups. Fill half of cup 1 with moist soil. Fill half of cup 2 with dry soil.

Using Math

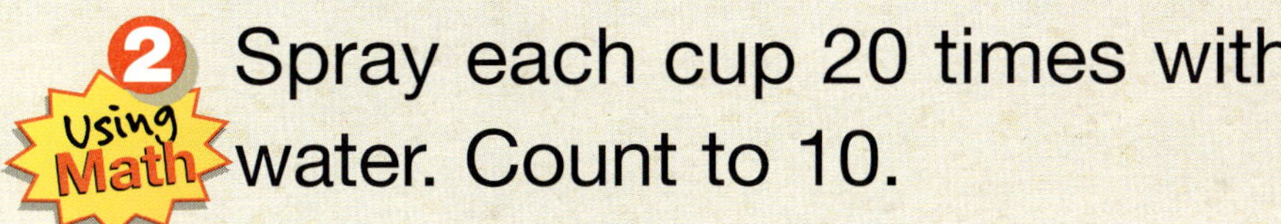

2 Spray each cup 20 times with water. Count to 10.

3 Repeat step 2.

4 **Record** what happens.

Think! What happened to the water in each cup? Why did this happen?

Find Out More!

Make a list of questions about plants and what they need to live. Then make a plan to find answers. Use the plan. Tell about what you find.

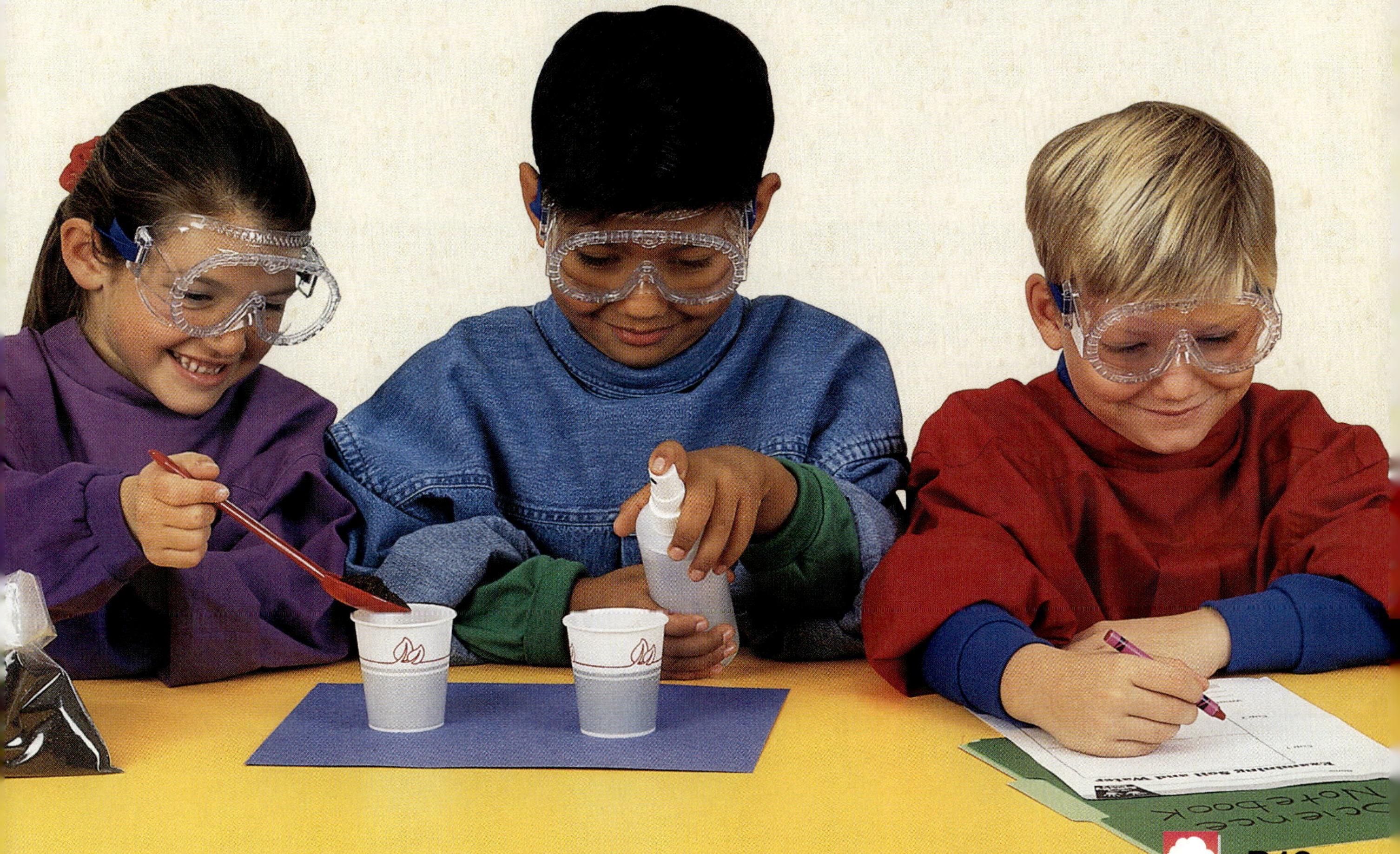

Water in Soil

Soil is made of tiny rocks and once-living things. There are many little spaces in soil. When it rains, water soaks into these spaces. If there is more water than the spaces in the soil can hold, puddles may form.

Over time, some water from the puddles goes into the air. Water from the puddles may also slowly soak into the soil. The water in the soil is used by living things. What living things use water in the soil?

Reading Check **Tell** what happens to soil after it rains. Why do puddles form?

How does water move?

Observing How Water Flows

1. Use wet sand to make a small hill in a pan.

2 Put a button in a place where you **predict** water will flow.

3 **Measure** one cup of water. Slowly pour the water from the measuring cup onto the top of the hill.

Using Math

4 **Watch** where the water flows. **Record** what you see.

Think! Where did the water flow?

Visit **www.eduplace.com** to learn about the ways we use water.

Moving Water

Water flows downhill. Sometimes it goes fast. Sometimes it goes slowly.

The first picture shows water moving downhill in a **river**. The water goes fast. When the water reaches the bottom, it goes slowly.

Moving water is very strong. It can cut a path in the ground. The middle picture shows moving water in a small river called a **stream**.

Water moves in an **ocean**, too. You can see ocean waves moving in the last picture.

Reading Check **Act out** how water moves. Where is moving water found?

Where does water gather?

Observing How Water Gathers

What You Need

 goggles

 soil

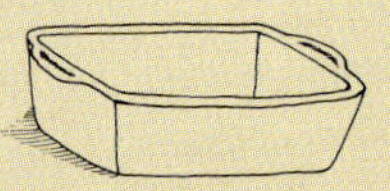 plastic dishpan

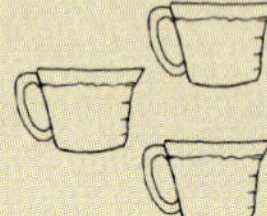 3 measuring cups of water

Science Notebook

1. Cover the bottom of a dishpan with soil. Push down the soil in the middle.

2 Slowly pour 3 cups of water into the dishpan. **Watch** where the water flows.

3 **Record** what you see.

Think! What happened to the water?

Puddles and Lakes

Water that doesn't soak into the ground forms a puddle. It can dry up in the sunshine.

Water from springs and rivers can form a lake. A **lake** has a lot of water in it. Most lakes do not dry up in the sunshine.

Look at the picture. Where is the river water flowing? It is flowing downhill into a lake.

Lakes need to be kept clean so that the water is safe to use. Then we can have fun there. How might you help keep a lake clean?

Reading Check **Draw a picture** that shows places where you have seen water gather.

CHECKPOINT

Word Power

If you need help, turn to the pages shown in blue.

Match a word with a picture. (D18–D19, D22–D23)

stream   river   lake

1.  **2.**  **3.** 

Use these words to fill in the blanks.

living   clay soil   once-living

4. A ______ thing needs air, water, and food to stay alive. (D8–D9)

5. Soil that is under topsoil is called ______. (D4–D5)

6. Fallen leaves are ______ things. (D8–D9)

Solving Science Problems

Look at the picture. Explain what the problem is. Then tell how you could help to solve the problem.

People Using Science

Ecologist

Ecologists study living things and the places where they live. Ecologists might study life underwater, in a rain forest, or in the air. They might study plants to find out where the plants live.

How can studying plants help an ecologist know where different kinds of bugs live?

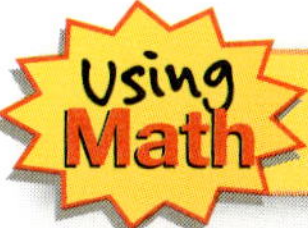

Make a Tally Chart

Make a tally chart like the one below. Then use the pictures to complete the chart.

Kinds of Things		
Thing	**Tally**	**Total**
Living		
Nonliving		
Once-living		

How can rocks be grouped?

Activity

Looking at Rocks

1. Spread out rocks on a table. **Look at** and feel each rock.

2. **Measure** the mass of each rock on a balance.

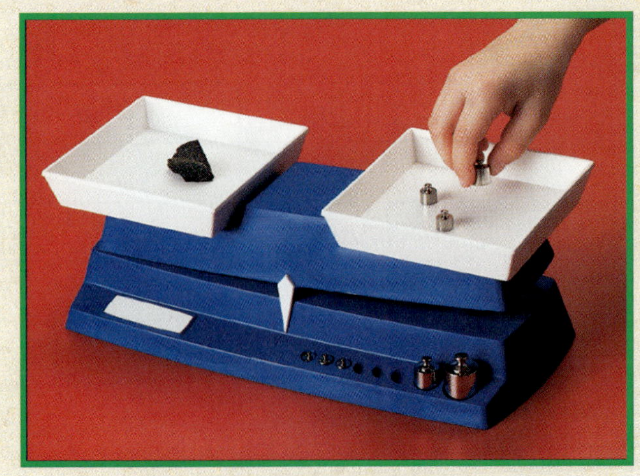

3 Decide how to **group** the rocks. Put each group on a paper plate. **Draw** each group.

Think! How did you group the rocks?

Internet Field Trip

Visit **www.eduplace.com** to learn more about rocks and minerals.

Grouping Rocks

Rocks come in many colors, shapes, and sizes. Look at the rocks in the picture. What color groups could you make? How would you group the rocks by shape? Which rocks would you group together by size?

Rocks can be grouped by the way they feel. Some rocks are smooth. Other rocks are not smooth. They are rough.

The white rock in the picture is rough. Which rocks are smooth?

Reading Check Make a group of rocks from the picture. **Write** about how the rocks are alike.

How can the hardness of rocks be compared?

Testing the Hardness of Rocks

What You Need

 goggles

  rocks

 tile

 Science Notebook

1. Spread rocks on a table.

2. Squeeze each rock in your hand. **Record** how each rock feels.

3. Use your fingernail to scratch each rock. **Record** what you **observe**.

4. Then scratch a tile with each rock. **Record** what you **observe.**

Testing Hardness of Rocks			
Rock 1			

5. **Compare** the rocks.

Think! Which rocks were the hardest? Tell how you know.

Looking at Hardness

Some rocks are harder than others. Hard rocks can **scratch**, or make a mark on, softer rocks. Soft rocks can't scratch harder rocks.

The pictures show two kinds of rocks. How can you tell which rock is harder?

The first artist is making powder from rock. The rock is soft. The artist uses the rock powder to make a picture.

The next artist is using harder rock. She uses a hammer to chip the rock. She chips away the rock to make a shape she likes.

Rocks are used for many things. Hard rocks and soft rocks have different uses.

◀ Graphite is not very hard. It is used in pencils.

Diamonds are the hardest rocks. They are used in jewelry. ▶

◀ Bauxite is used to make aluminum. Aluminum is used to make foil and baking pans.

Talc is the softest rock. It is used to make baby powder. ▶

Using Math Look at the table. The highest numbers show the hardest rocks.

Hardness of Rocks				
	Bauxite	**Diamond**	**Graphite**	**Talc**
Hardness	3	10	2	1

Use the table to answer the questions.

1. Which rock is harder than bauxite?
2. Can graphite scratch bauxite? Tell how you know.
3. Put the rocks in order from softest to hardest.

Reading Check **Write** about the different ways the hardness of rocks can be compared.

LESSON 8

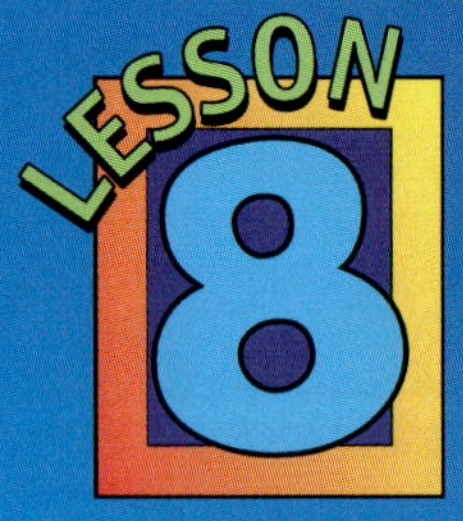

How large are rocks?

Activity

Examining Sizes of Rocks

What You Need

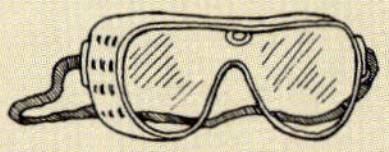 goggles

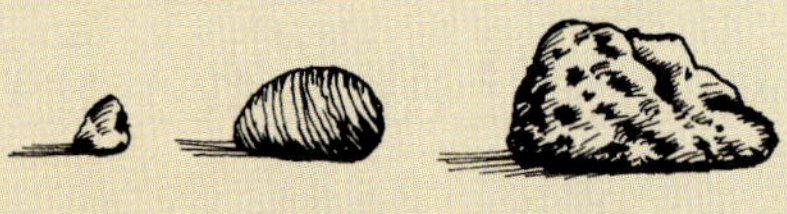 rocks

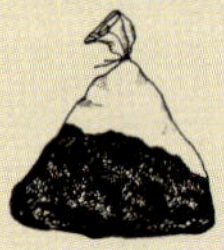 sand

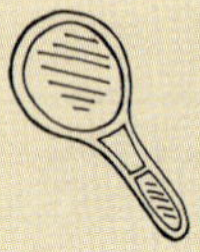 hand lens

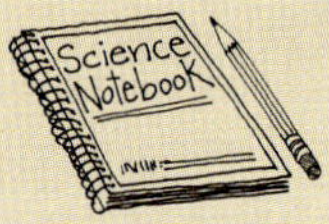

Science Notebook

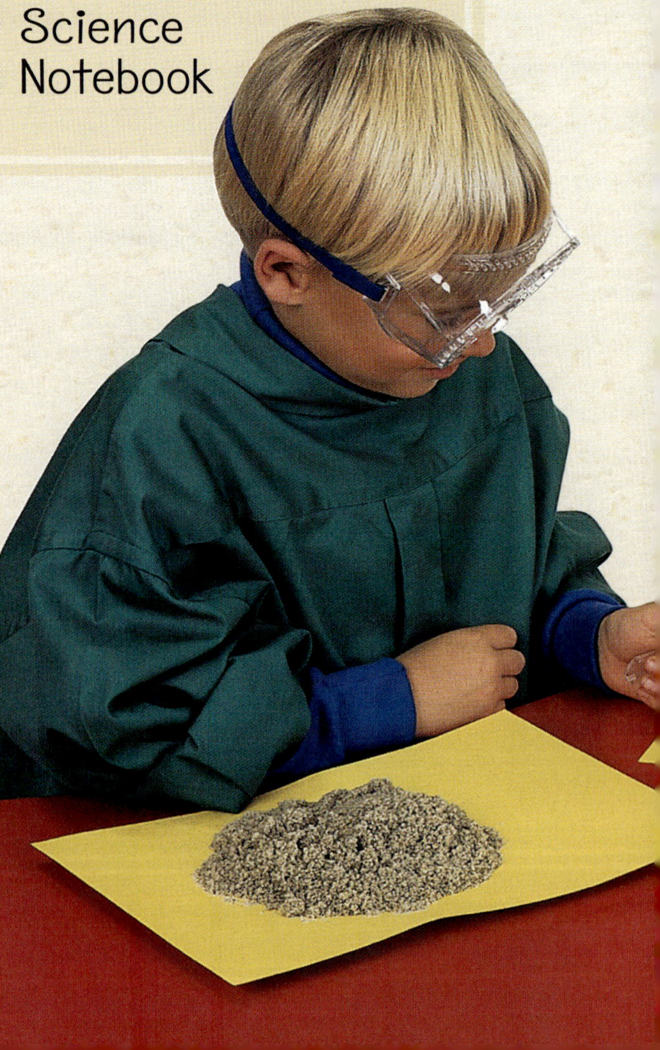

1. Spread rocks and sand on a table.

2. **Look at** each rock with a hand lens. **Draw** what you see.

3 **Look at** the sand with a hand lens. **Draw** what you see.

Think! How are the rocks and the sand alike, and how are they different?

Find Out More!

How many pieces of rock are in a pinch of sand? Make a plan to find the answer. What tools will you need? Compare your findings with those of other groups.

Looking at Size

Rocks come in many sizes. Very big rocks are called **boulders**.

The picture shows rocks of different sizes. The very big rock in the front is a boulder. It is the biggest rock in the picture.

After a long time, moving water wears away rocks. The water makes the rocks smaller. What might you find on the bottom of the river? You might find small rocks and sand. **Sand** is made up of tiny pieces of rock.

Reading Check **Tell a story** about rocks in a river. Use the words big, small, tiny, and boulder.

How does recycling help the earth?

Activity

Making Compost

1. Fill two cartons with soil.
2. Bury a piece of banana peel in carton 1 and a cap in carton 2.
3. Using Math: Spray each carton 10 times and then close each carton. Put both cartons in a warm place.

4. Repeat step 3 each day for four weeks.

5. Uncover the objects once a week and **record** what you see.

Think! How did the objects change?

Find Out More!

CD-ROM

Composting is a way of recycling. Listen to **Science Blaster Jr.** to hear more ways to recycle.

Using Soil, Rocks, and Water

Recycling means using things again. This woman is making compost. **Compost** is something made by recycling once-living things. Look at the large photo. The woman is adding fruit and vegetable scraps to the pile.

Look at the small photos. The woman mixes leaves and grass clippings with the scraps. Then she stirs the pile. In time these things will break down to become compost.

The woman adds the compost to the soil. Soil is used to help plants grow.

There are many ways to recycle. Even rocks can be recycled. Look at the pictures.

▲ Boulders were found at a building site. A wall was built with these huge rocks.

▲ An old road was crushed to make gravel. These little rocks are under the new road.

Many cities recycle water. Dirty water is sent to a water-treatment place. After the water has been cleaned, it is used to water grass.

Reading Check **Tell** how recycling food scraps, rocks, and water can help the earth.

UNIT D

UNIT REVIEW

Word Power

If you need help, turn to the pages shown in blue.

Match the words with a picture. (D8–D9, D38–D39)

boulder sand living thing

1. 

2. 

3. 

Write the letter of the correct word.

4. When you use things again, you ______. (D42–D43)

a. stream **b.** rock **c.** scratch **d.** recycle

5. Water in an ______ moves in waves. (D18–D19)

a. puddle **b.** ocean **c.** sand **d.** downhill

6. Hard rocks can ______ softer rocks. (D32–D33)

a. clay **b.** topsoil **c.** scratch **d.** compost

7. The top layer of soil is called ______. (D4–D5)

a. topsoil **b.** clay **c.** sand **d.** rock

8. You can recycle fruit and vegetable scraps into ______. (D42–D43)

a. rock **b.** clay **c.** scratch **d.** compost

Using Science Ideas

Look at the picture. List the living things you see. Next, list the once-living things you see. Then list the nonliving things you see.

Writing in Science

A space explorer has found a rock on the moon. You are a newspaper reporter. You need to learn about the moon rock. Make a list of questions to ask about the moon rock.

Reading Skills

Cause and Effect

When the rain stopped, Todd went outside. He wanted to see how the rain changed the soil and rocks. Look at the picture. Make a list of the changes Todd found.

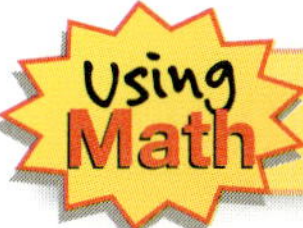 Guess and Check

About how many paper clips long is each rock?
Guess. Then use paper clips to measure.

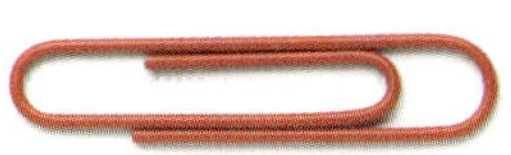

1. 

Guess

about ______ clips

Measure

about ______ clips

2. 

Guess

about ______ clips

Measure

about ______ clips

3. 

Guess

about ______ clips

Measure

about ______ clips

Keeping Fit and Healthy

Themes: Systems; Constancy and Change

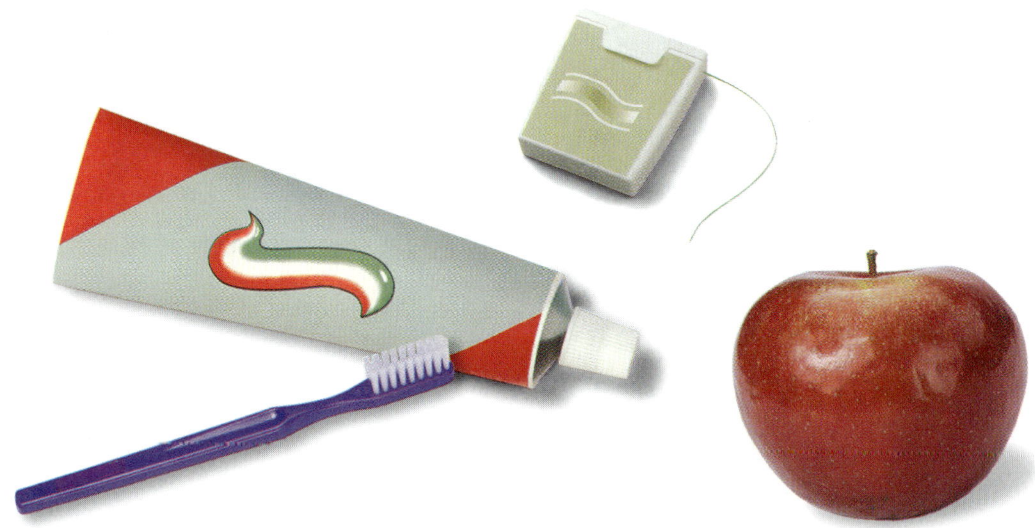

What kinds of food does your body need?

Activity

Grouping Foods

What You Need

empty food containers

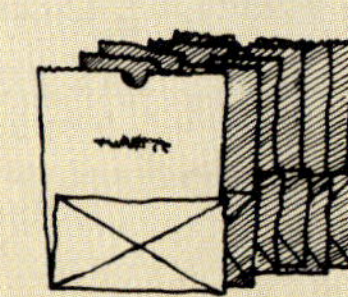
6 grocery bags with labels

Science Notebook

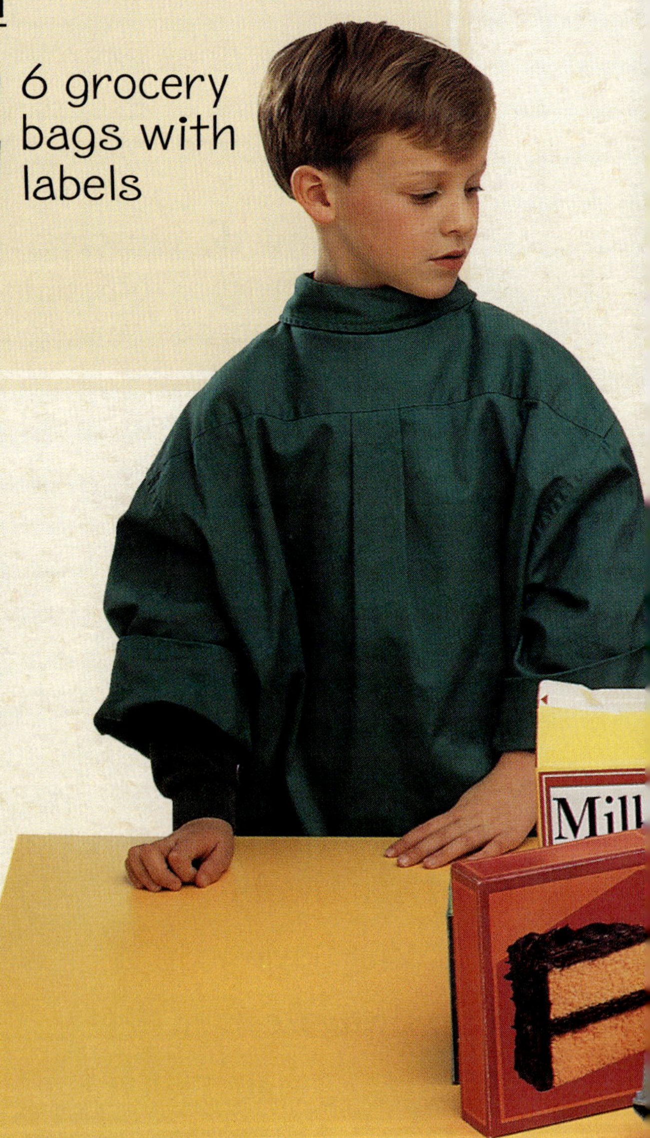

1. Bring in empty food containers from home.
2. **Sort** the containers into food groups. Using Math
3. **Draw a picture** of the food in each group. Name each food.

4. Think of other foods to add to these groups. **Tell** why you think they belong.

Think! What kinds of foods should you eat the most? Tell how you decided.

Find Out More!

CD-ROM

Use **Science Blaster Jr.** Go to the Engineering Room to sort out food groups. Collect fruits, vegetables, snacks, and more.

The Food Pyramid

The picture shows a **food pyramid**. It tells about the foods you need each day to stay healthy. The food pyramid tells how many servings of different types of food your body needs.

A roll is one **serving** of bread. An apple is one serving of fruit. You need more servings of some foods than others.

You should eat three to five servings of vegetables each day. What foods do you need two to four servings of each day?

There are six food groups in the food pyramid. A **food group** has like kinds of food. Milk, yogurt, and cheese are one food group. This group has things that are made with milk. What other foods belong to this group?

The box at the bottom of the pyramid is the largest. Your body needs the most servings from this food group. The smallest box is at the top of the pyramid. Your body needs the fewest servings from this food group.

Reading Check **List** the six food groups. Name some of your favorite foods in each group.

LESSON 2

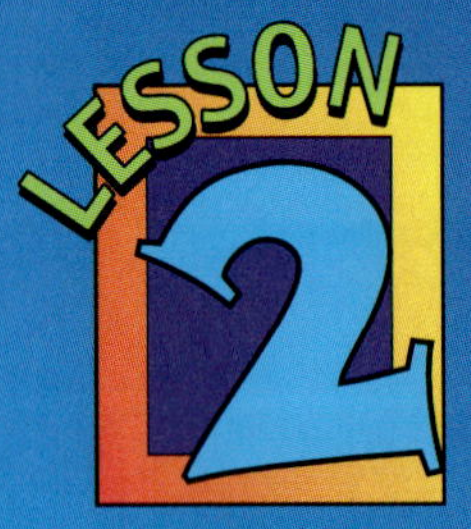

What is a balanced meal?

Activity

Fishing for a Balanced Meal

What You Need

- food pictures
- scissors
- glue
- paper fish
- paper clips
- paper fish pond
- magnet on a string
- Science Notebook

1. Cut out pictures of food. Glue each picture to a paper fish.

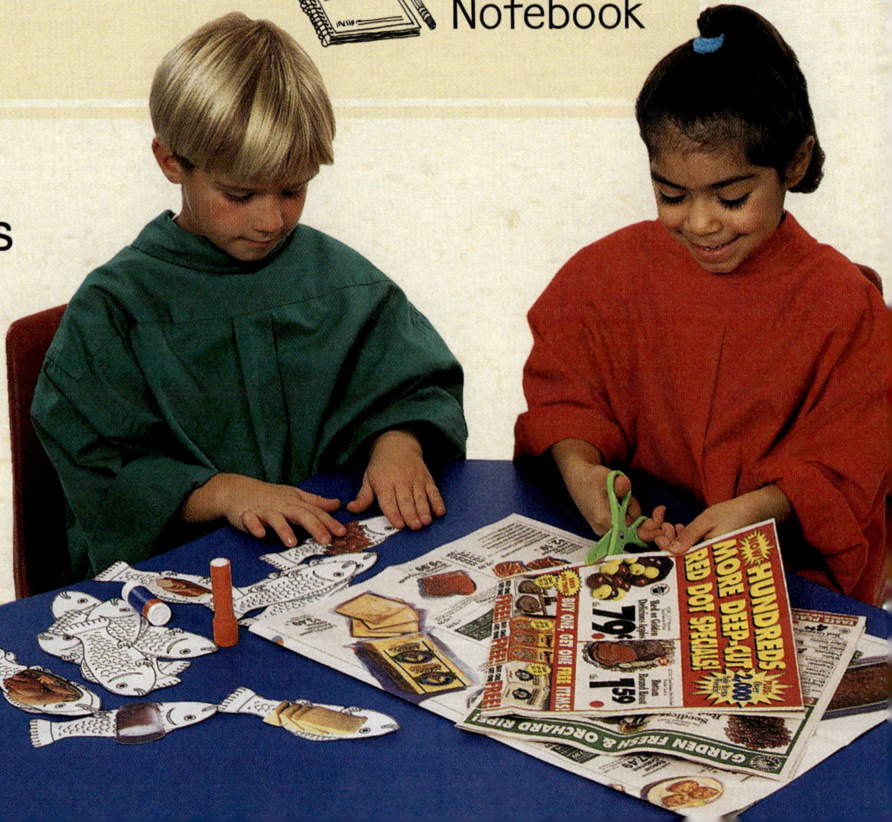

2 Put a paper clip on each fish. Put your fish in a paper pond.

3 Use the magnet to fish for a balanced meal.

4 **Record** your meal by gluing your fish onto your plate.

Think! What makes a meal balanced?

Visit **www.eduplace.com** to learn more about your favorite foods.

Combining Foods

Many people eat three meals a day. They eat breakfast early in the day. They eat lunch in the middle of the day. They eat dinner late in the day.

A **balanced meal** has food from many food groups. It has few fats or sweets.

The pictures show balanced meals. The first meal has food from three food groups.

The cereal is from one group. The milk in the pitcher is from another group. The fruit and juice are from a third group.

Reading Check **Draw a picture** of a balanced meal. Which food group is each food from?

Which foods make healthful snacks?

Testing Snack Foods

1. Write **oil** on one paper square. Put a drop of oil on that square.

2 Write the name of each food on a different paper square. Rub each square with the food it names.

3 Hold each square up to the light. **Compare** each square to the square with oil. **Record** what you see.

Think! Which snacks are more healthful than others? Tell why you think so.

Good Snacks

Food you eat between meals is a **snack**. Some snacks are good for your body. Some are not.

There are snacks that have a lot of fat and oil in them. Potato chips and doughnuts have fat and oil in them.

The picture shows many foods. These foods make healthful snacks. Fruits are good snacks. Vegetables are good snacks. Snacks can be from more than one food group, too.

Pretend you are making a healthful snack. What would you put on the plate?

The pictures show good snacks from different parts of the world.

▲ This Russian bread can be filled with meat, fish, eggs, or vegetables.

▲ People in Lebanon serve these yogurt and vegetable dips with pita bread.

▲ People in Mexico eat nachos as a snack.

Make a card like the one below. It shows what you need to make 2 servings of nachos. Double the amounts to show what you need for 4 servings.

NACHOS

Food	2 Servings	4 Servings
Tomatoes	1	2
Green Onions	1	
Shredded Cheese	5 tablespoons	
Tortilla Chips	6	

Reading Check **Draw a picture** to show healthful snacks you and your friends enjoy.

CHECKPOINT

Word Power

If you need help, turn to the pages shown in blue.

Match the words with a picture. (E4–E7, E10–E11)

balanced meal   food group   food pyramid

1. 

2. 

3. 

Use these words to fill in the blanks.

serving   snack   balanced

4. Food you eat between meals is a _____. (E14–E15)

5. An apple is one _____ of fruit. (E4–E5)

6. A meal with food from different food groups is a _____ meal. (E10–E11)

Solving Science Problems

Look at the list of foods. What would you choose for a balanced meal? Tell why.

milk	grapes	cheese sandwich
fish sticks	cookie	carrot sticks
popcorn	yogurt	ham sandwich
peanuts	peach	noodles and cheese

People Using Science

Dietitian

A dietitian talks with people about the kinds of food they need and how much food they need to stay healthy.

Dietitians work in places like hospitals and schools to plan healthful meals.

Where else might a dietitian be useful?

Using Math Using a Bar Graph

A class made a graph of their favorite fruits.

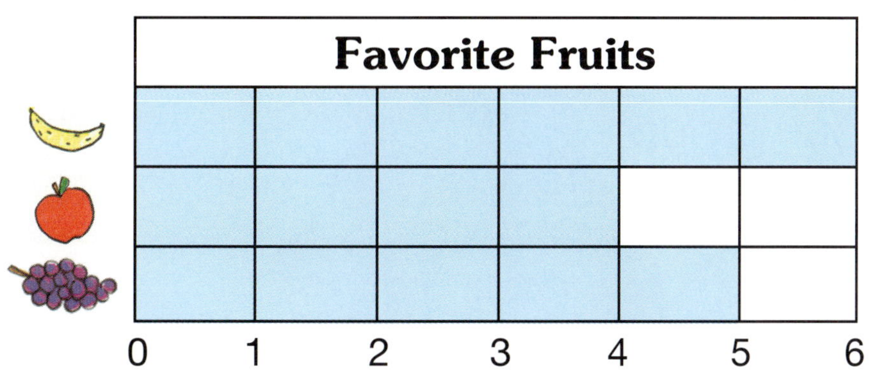

Use the graph to answer the questions.

1. How many children like best?
2. How many children like and in all?
3. How many more children like than ?

How does exercise help your body?

Exercising Our Muscles

What You Need

6 exercise cards

Science Notebook

1. Choose an exercise card. Show the card to your group.

2. Do the exercise with your group.

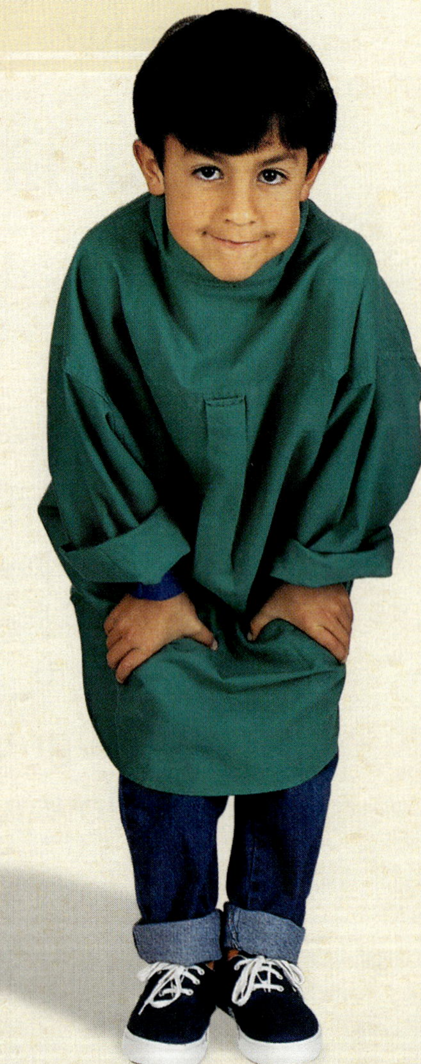

3. **Talk about** which muscle you used the most. **Record** your ideas.

Exercising Muscles	
Exercise	**Which muscles we use the most**
crunches	
knee bends	

4. Repeat steps 1–3, using the other exercise cards.

Think! How do your muscles feel after you exercise them?

Find Out More!

Ask your classmates questions about their favorite ways to exercise. Make a tally chart to record your data. Then put the data into a bar graph.

Moving Muscles

You have bones in your body. You have muscles in your body. **Muscles** help you move.

As you move, you **exercise** your muscles. Exercise makes muscles and bones stronger. Exercise helps your body stay healthy.

Look at the pictures. The children are playing. They are moving in different ways. The boy is jumping rope. He is using the muscles in his arms and legs. What are the other children doing? What muscles are they using?

Reading Check **Write a story** about friends exercising to stay healthy.

How do muscles and bones work together?

Measuring Muscles

What You Need

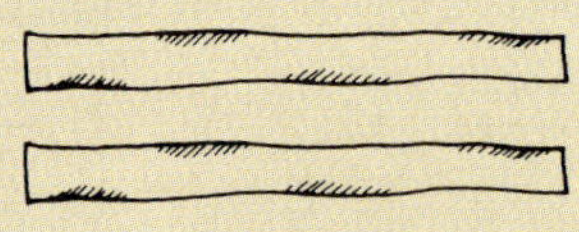
2 construction paper strips

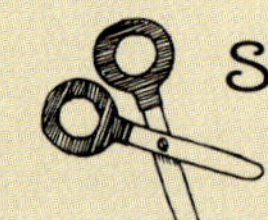
scissors

glue

Science Notebook

1 Put your arms at your sides. Have your partners **measure** around your upper arm with a paper strip. Mark the length.

2. Take the paper strip off your arm. Cut the strip at the mark. Glue the strip on a chart.

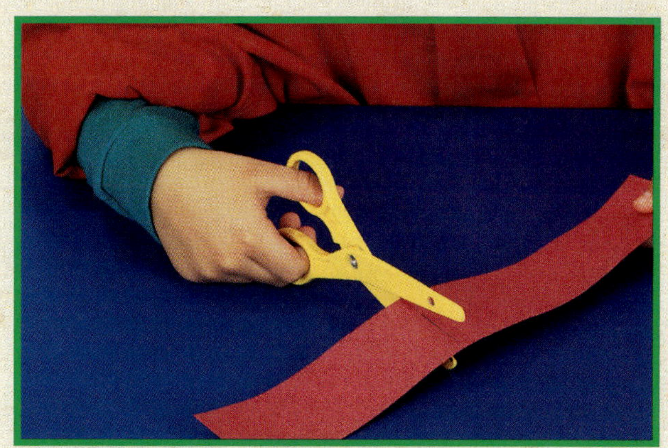

3. Make a muscle. Have your partners **measure** your arm again with another paper strip. Mark the length.

4. Cut the paper strip at the mark. Glue the strip on the chart. **Compare** the strips. **Record** your findings.

Think! How did the size of your arm muscle change? Why did this happen?

Muscles and Bones

Look at the pictures. The children are making funny faces. They are moving their muscles to make faces.

Muscles and bones work together. Muscles pull on bones to make the bones move.

Muscles in your face can help show how you feel. Make a face that shows you are happy. Feel the muscles and bones that make your face move. Do the same thing for a sad face. Compare how your muscles moved each time.

Reading Check Use your muscles and bones together. **Act out** your favorite animal.

Why do you need sleep?

Activity
Recording My Sleep

What You Need

Science Notebook

1. Find out how many hours you slept last night.
2. Color one box on a graph for every hour you slept. *Using Math*
3. Repeat steps 1 and 2 for each night.
4. **Record** how you felt before going to sleep and after waking up.

Think! **How much sleep do you need? Tell why you think so.**

Find Out More!

Look at your graph. Predict how much sleep other children your age need. Plan a way to show how many hours most children sleep. Tell about what you find.

Rest and Sleep

Look at the pictures. Follow the boy through his busy day. First, the boy walks to school. He is getting exercise.

Next, the boy does work at school. Then he plays outside. After that, he rests a little.

You **rest** by sitting or lying down quietly. What things does the boy do after he rests?

Look at the last picture. The boy is sleeping. Your body rests when you **sleep** at night. You need rest and sleep to stay healthy.

Reading Check **Tell** about ways you rest each day. Why are rest and sleep important?

What are good health habits?

Observing Clean and Dirty Hands

1. **Predict** whether your hands are clean or dirty. **Record** your prediction.

2. Wipe your hands with a wet wipe. **Record** what you find out.

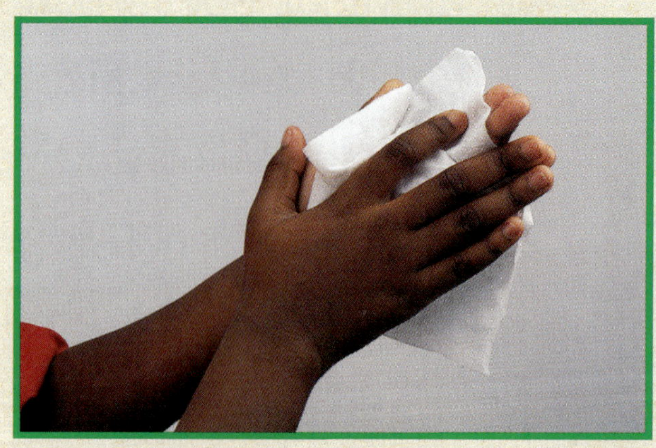

3. Wash your hands with soap and water. Then rinse and dry your hands.

4. Wipe your hands again with another wet wipe. **Record** what you find out.

Think! Why is washing your hands with soap and water important?

Good Health Habits

Germs can make you sick. They are very small. You can't see germs. But they are all around.

Good health habits help you stay well. You can wash with soap to kill germs. You can use a tissue to keep germs from spreading.

Look at the picture. Find people who are showing good health habits. Can you find the boy who is using a tissue when he sneezes?

Now find people who are not showing good health habits. What are they doing?

Reading Check **Write** a list of good health habits. Share the list with a classmate.

How can you keep teeth healthy?

Brushing Out Stains

1. Put 2 or 3 drops of grape juice on two tiles. Let the tiles dry.

2 Use a toothbrush to brush tile 1. **Record** what happens.

3 Put toothpaste on the brush. Brush tile 2. **Record** what happens.

Think! Which tile was easier to clean? Tell why you think so.

Internet Field Trip

Visit **www.eduplace.com** to learn more about teeth.

Caring for Teeth

Cleaning your teeth keeps them strong and healthy. Eating balanced meals also helps keep your teeth strong and healthy.

Look at the picture. The girl wants strong and healthy teeth. What things will help her?

She can eat an apple. It is a healthful food. She can **brush** her teeth with a toothbrush and toothpaste. She can use thin string called **floss** to clean between her teeth.

What things are not good for her teeth? Candy and other sweets are not good for teeth.

A trip to the dentist's office can help keep your teeth healthy. A dental hygienist might take pictures that show what is inside your teeth. Then he or she will clean your teeth.

The dentist looks at the pictures. Then the dentist fixes any teeth that need it.

◀ **dental hygienist**

dentist ▶

Have you lost any teeth? Many children start losing their baby teeth when they are about six years old. You need to keep your mouth clean even when you lose some teeth. That gives your new teeth a healthy place to grow.

Reading Check **Tell a story** about a tooth. How does its owner keep it healthy?

UNIT E

Unit Review

Word Power

If you need help, turn to the pages shown in blue.

Match a word with a picture. (E22, E31, E39)

sleep exercise brush

1.

2.

3.

Write the letter of the correct word.

4. You use a thin string called _____ to clean between your teeth. (E38–E39)

a. floss **b.** rest **c.** brush **d.** food

5. Your _____ help you move your body. (E22–E23)

a. rest **b.** sleep **c.** muscles **d.** germs

6. You _____ by sitting or lying down quietly. (E30–E31)

a. brush **b.** rest **c.** muscles **d.** exercise

7. Good _____ help you stay well. (E34–E35)

a. floss **b.** brush **c.** serving **d.** health habits

8. The _____ tells how many servings of food your body needs. (E4–E5)

a. dentist **b.** rest **c.** healthful **d.** food pyramid

Using Science Ideas

How is running helping to keep these men fit and healthy?

Writing in Science

Look at the picture. Is this a healthful meal? How could you make it more healthful? List the foods in your more healthful meal.

Main Idea

Read the story below. Then choose the sentence that tells the main idea.

Good health habits help your body stay well. Exercise makes your muscles and bones stronger. Washing your hands helps keep germs from spreading. Brushing and flossing help keep your teeth strong. Rest and sleep help your body, too.

a. Exercise makes your muscles and bones stronger.

b. Good health habits help your body stay well.

c. Rest and sleep help your body, too.

d. Washing your hands helps keep germs from spreading.

Using Math: Using a Schedule

Bill's Morning Schedule

Time	Activity
7:00	get dressed
7:30	eat breakfast
8:00	brush teeth
8:30	walk to school

Use the schedule to answer the questions.

1. What does Bill do at 8:30?
2. At what time does Bill get dressed?
3. Does Bill brush his teeth before or after he eats breakfast?
4. At what time does Bill eat breakfast?

Science and Math Toolbox

Using a Hand Lens

A hand lens is a tool that makes objects look bigger. It helps you see the small parts of an object.

Look at a Coin

1. Place a coin on your desk.

2. Hold the hand lens above the coin. Look through the lens. Slowly move the lens away from the coin. What do you see?

3. Keep moving the lens away until the coin looks blurry.

4. Then slowly move the lens closer. Stop when the coin does not look blurry.

Using a

Thermometer

A thermometer is a tool used to measure temperature. Temperature tells how hot or cold something is. It is measured in degrees.

Find the Temperature of Water

1. Put water into a cup.
2. Put a thermometer into the cup.
3. Watch the colored liquid in the thermometer. What do you see?
4. Look how high the colored liquid is. What number is closest? That is the temperature of the water.

Using a Ruler

A ruler is a tool used to measure the length of objects. Some rulers measure length in inches. Other rulers measure length in centimeters.

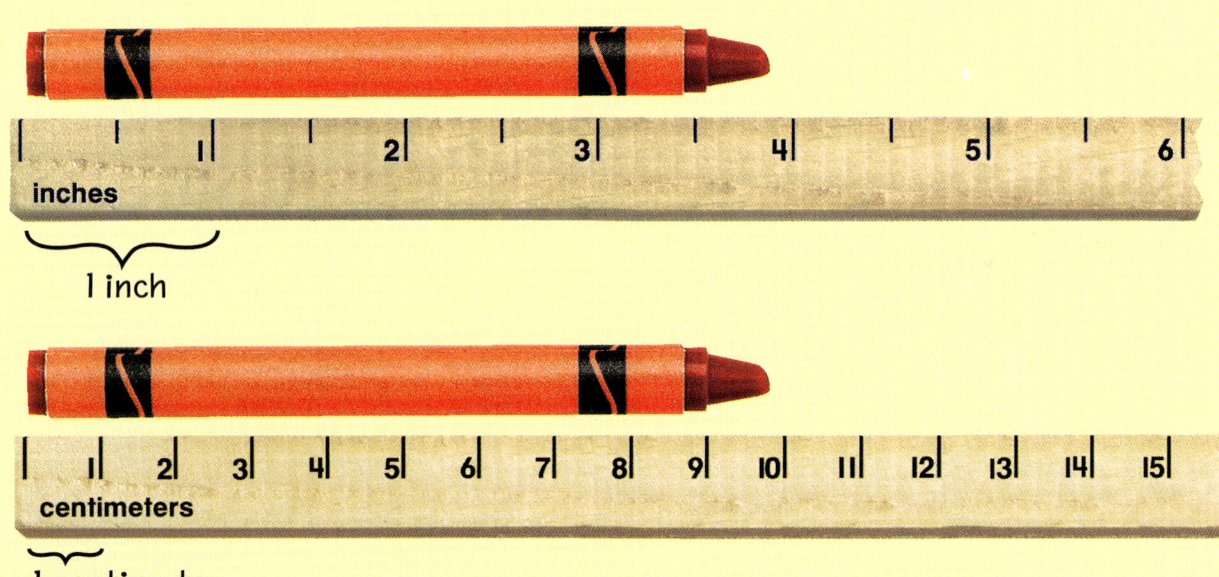

Measure a Crayon

1. Place the ruler on your desk.

2. Lay your crayon next to the ruler. Line up one end with the 0 mark on the ruler.

3. Look at the other end of the crayon. Which number is closest to that end?

Using a
Calculator

A calculator is a tool that can help you add numbers. It can also help you subtract numbers.

Subtract Numbers

1. Tim and Anna both grew plants.
   Tim grew 8 plants.
   Anna grew 17 plants.

2. How many more plants did Anna grow?
   Use your calculator to find out.

3. Enter 1 7 on the calculator.
   Then press the − key.
   Enter 8 and press =.

4. What is your answer?

Using a Balance

A balance is a tool used to measure mass. Mass is the amount of matter in an object.

Measure the Mass of Clay

1. Check that the pointer is on the middle mark of the balance. If needed, move the slider on the back to the left or right.
2. Place a clay ball in one pan.
3. Add masses to the other pan until the pointer is at the middle mark again.
4. Add the numbers on the masses to find the mass in grams of the clay.
5. Add more clay to the ball. Repeat steps 3 and 4. How did the mass change?

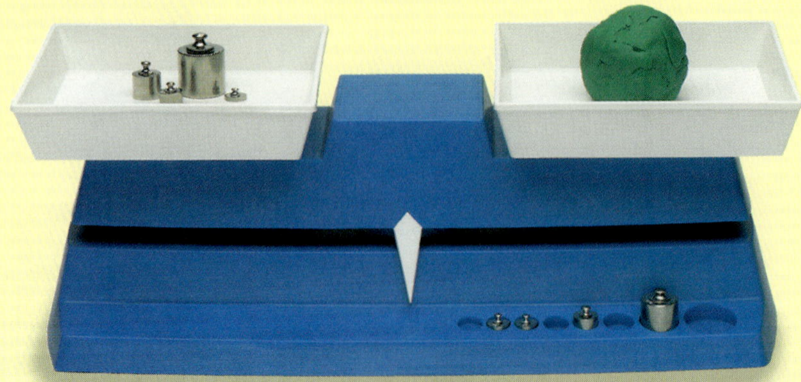

Making a Chart

A chart can help you sort information, or data. When you sort data it is easier to read and compare.

Make a Chart to Compare Animals

1. Give the chart a title.
2. Name the groups that tell about the data you collect.
3. Carefully fill in the data in each column.

How Animals Move	
Animal	**How it moves**
fish	swim
dog	walk, swim
duck	walk, swim, fly

Which animal can move in the most ways?

Making a Tally Chart

A tally chart helps you keep track of items as you count.

Make a Tally Chart of Kinds of Pets

Jan's class drew pictures of their pets. You can make a tally chart to record the number of each kind of pet.

1. Every time you count one pet, you make one tally.

2. When you get to five, your fifth tally should be a line across the other four.

3. Count the tallies to find each total.

Kinds of Pets

Pet	Tally	Total
Bird	III	3
Dog	~~IIII~~ I	6
Fish	I	1

How many of each kind of pet do the children have?

Making a

Bar Graph

A bar graph can help you sort and compare data.

Favorite Leaves		
Leaf	**Tally**	**Total**
Oak	IIII	4
Ash	~~IIII~~ I	6
Maple	II	2
Birch	III	3

Make a Bar Graph of Favorite Leaves

You can use the data in the tally chart to make a bar graph.

1. Choose a title for your graph.
2. Write numbers along the side.
3. Write leaf names along the bottom.
4. Start at the bottom of each column. Fill in one box for each tally.

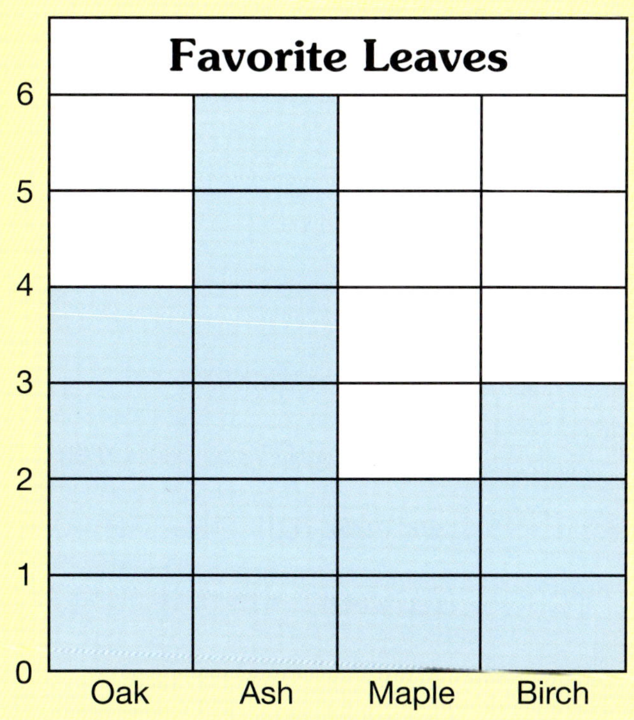

Which leaf is the favorite?

GLOSSARY

A

animals Living things. They can move from place to place. Animals have body coverings. They eat other animals or plants for food. (A16)

attract To pull toward itself. A magnet attracts things made of iron, steel, and nickel. (C4)

autumn The season of the year that comes before winter. Leaves fall off many trees in autumn. (B33)

B

balanced meal Includes foods from most of the food groups on the food pyramid. (E10)

bar magnet A long, straight piece of steel that has been magnetized. A bar magnet attracts things made of iron, steel, and nickel. (C14)

bird A two-legged animal with feathers and wings. A bird is the only animal that has feathers covering its body. (A42)

boulder A very large rock. (D38)

breeze A gentle wind. The breeze makes a flag wave slowly. (B19)

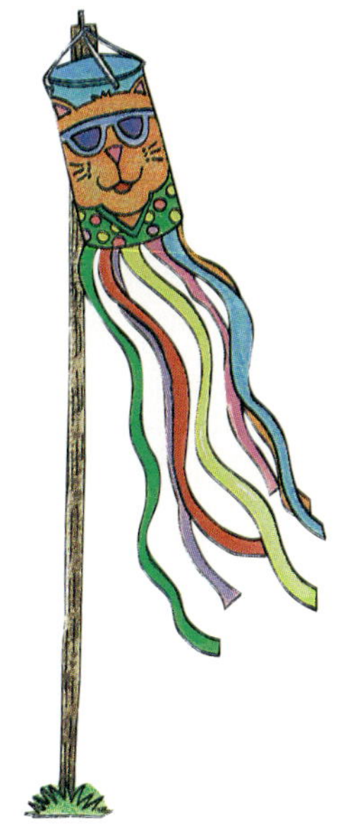

brush To clean one's teeth. When you brush your teeth, you remove food bits from them. (E39)

C

calm When the wind is calm, no wind is blowing. (B19)

clay soil Soil that has a lot of clay in it. Clay soil is found below topsoil. (D5)

cloud A group of tiny drops of water in the air. Rain falls from some clouds. (B26)

compass A tool that is used to show direction. The needle of a compass always points north. (C39)

compost Made by recycling once-living things. It can be added to soil to help plants grow. (D42)

cone The part of some nonflowering plants where seeds grow. Seeds grow between the scales of a cone. (A12)

E

exercise Moving your body. Playing outdoors is good exercise. (E22)

F

feathers Body covering of birds. Feathers keep birds warm. (A23)

fish An animal that lives in water. It has gills for breathing and fins for swimming. Many fish have scales. (A42)

floss Thin string used to clean between teeth. Flossing removes food a toothbrush cannot reach. (E39)

flower A part of some plants. Seeds form in a flower. (A8)

fog A group of tiny drops of water in the air. Fog is a cloud close to the ground. (B26)

food group A group of like kinds of food. Apples and bananas are part of the same food group. (E6)

food pyramid Shows the different food groups. The food pyramid also shows how many servings of each group you should eat each day. (E4)

good health habits Habits that help you stay well. Washing your hands before you eat is a good health habit. (E34)

hair Body covering of mammals. Hair helps mammals stay warm and protects their skin. (A22)

heat One kind of energy. The heat from the sun warms the earth. (B14)

hibernate To sleep through the winter. Some squirrels hibernate. (B43)

ice Water that is in the form of a solid. Ice is hard and cold. (B24)

lake A body of water with land all around it. Water flows into lakes from rivers. (D22)

leaves Parts of plants. Leaves make food for the plants. Leaves grow on stems or up from the roots. (A9)

life cycle The order of changes that occur during the lifetime of living things. Plants and animals have life cycles. (A46)

like poles Two south poles or two north poles of different magnets. Like poles repel each other. (C23)

living thing Something that is alive. Living things need air, water, and food to grow. (D9)

magnet A piece of metal that attracts things made of iron, steel, and nickel. (C4)

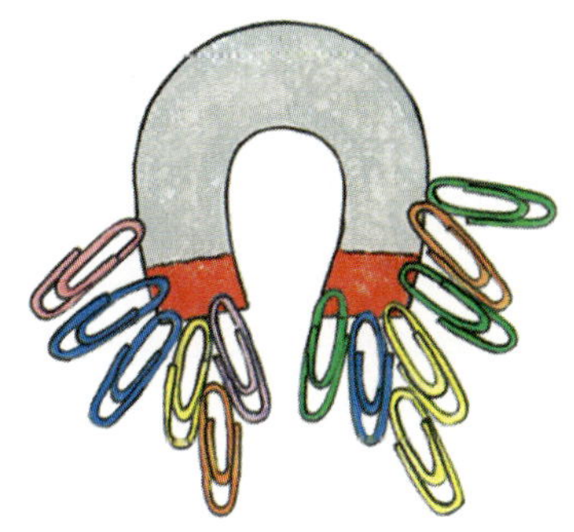

magnetic field The area around a magnet. It is where the force of the magnet works. (C28)

magnetic force A force that attracts things made of steel, iron, or nickel to a magnet. Magnetic force can go through air. (C8)

mammal One kind of animal. Mammals are covered with hair. They feed milk to their babies. (A40)

meat eater An animal that eats other animals. Meat eaters have sharp teeth to tear their food into pieces. (A35)

migrate To move from place to place as the seasons change. Some birds migrate south for the winter. (B42)

muscles Body parts that help you move. The muscles in your legs help you run and jump. (E22)

needles Thin and pointed leaves. The shape of needles helps keep water in the plant. (A13)

nonliving thing
Something that was never alive. A rock is a nonliving thing. (D9)

ocean A great body of salt water. An ocean is larger than a lake. (D19)

once-living thing
Something that was alive at one time or was once part of a living thing. A feather and an acorn are once-living things. (D8)

plants Living things that need water, light, and air to grow. Most plants have roots, stems, and leaves. Many have flowers. (A8)

plant eater An animal that eats plants. A plant eater has flat teeth for grinding food. (A35)

poles The places on a magnet where the magnetic force is strongest. On a bar magnet, the poles are at the ends of the magnet. (C17)

recycling Using something again. Compost is made by recycling once-living things. (D42)

repel To push away or force apart. Like poles of two magnets repel each other. (C23)

rest To lie down or sit quietly. After you exercise, you should rest. (E31)

ring magnet A round, flat piece of metal that has been magnetized. It has a hole in the middle. The poles of a ring magnet are on the two flat sides. (C15)

river A body of water. It flows in a long path. Rivers flow downhill into lakes and oceans. (D18)

root A plant part. Roots grow down into the soil. Roots take in water from the soil. (A9)

sand Very small rocks. Some ocean beaches are covered with sand. (D39)

scales Body covering of some fish and reptiles. Scales are thin and flat. (A23)

scratch To make a mark on something. A harder rock will scratch a softer rock. (D32)

season A time of the year. Spring, summer, autumn, and winter are the four seasons. (B32)

serving The right amount of a food that you should eat. A serving of cereal may be 1 cup. (E5)

shade An area that is out of the sun. It is often cooler in the shade. (B11)

shelter A safe place to live. A nest is shelter for a bird. (A29)

skin A covering for the bodies of animals. Skin can be protected by hair, feathers, or scales. (A22)

sleep A period of rest. When you sleep, your body refreshes itself. (E31)

snack Food you eat between meals. Fruits are healthful snacks. Potato chips and candy are unhealthful snacks. (E14)

spring A season of the year. It comes after winter. In spring many plants begin to grow. (B33)

stem A plant part. Water and food move through stems. Some stems are hard. (A9)

stream A narrow path of flowing water. Streams are smaller than rivers. (D19)

strong wind A wind that blows fast and hard. A strong wind will blow paper down the street. (B19)

summer The season that comes after spring. Summer is the warmest season. Days are longer in the summer. (B33)

sunlight The light of the sun. Sunlight warms the earth. (B11)

temperature The measure of heat in an object. Temperature is measured by using a thermometer. (B5)

temporary magnet A magnet that works only for a short time. A temporary magnet can be made by stroking a metal object with a magnet. (C34)

topsoil The top part of soil. Topsoil is the part of soil in which most plants grow. Worms live in topsoil. (D5)

unlike poles The south pole and the north pole of different magnets. Unlike poles attract each other. (C22)

water vapor Water that is in the form of a gas. You cannot see water vapor. (B24)

weather What the air outside is like. Weather changes from day to day. (B4)

wind Fast-moving or slow-moving air. Wind can make objects move. (B18)

winter The season that comes after autumn. It is the coldest of the four seasons. Days are short in the winter. (B33)

INDEX

C

D

E

F

N

O

P

Q

R

S

T

U

W

CREDITS

ILLUSTRATORS
Cover: Liisa Chauncy Guida. **Think Like a Scientist:** 2–7: Benton Mahan. 10–11: Laurie Hamilton. *border:* Liisa Chauncy Guida.

Unit A: 1: Bob Pepper. 4–5: Dave Schweitzer. 12–13: Anne Feiza. 16–17: Bob Pepper. 18–19: Sharon Hawkins Vargo. 28–31: Patrick Gnan. 34–35: Randy Hamblin. 36–37: Phil Wilson. 46–47: Robert Roper. 48: Sharon Hawkins Vargo. 51: Liisa Chauncy Guida.

Unit B: B: Sharon Hawkins Vargo. 1: Nancy Tobin. 4–5: Nancy Tobin. 6: Andrew Shiff. 10–11: John Jones. 20–21: Denise and Fernando. 28: Sharon Hawkins Vargo. 32–33: Ellen Appleby. 48: Sharon Hawkins Vargo. 50: Jim Durk. 51: Saul Rosenbaum.

Unit C: C: Jerry Pavey. 1: *t.* Jerry Pavey, *b.* Sharon Hawkins Vargo. 18: *t.* Sharon Hawkins Vargo, *b.* Dorothy Stott. 22–23: *background* Julie Carpenter, *wooden toys* Jerry Pavey. 40, 43: Sharon Hawkins Vargo.

Unit D: 4–5, 14–15: Robert Roper. 22–23: Rose Mary Berlin. 24–25: Sharon Hawkins Vargo. 45: Nathan Young Jarvis. 46: Sharon Hawkins Vargo. 48: Julie Durrell.

Unit E: 4–7: Dan Brawer. 17–19: Sharon Hawkins Vargo. 30–31: Barbara Gray. 34–35: Jenny Campbell. 38–39: Ruth Flanigan. 42–43: Sharon Hawkins Vargo. 44: Susan Drawbaugh. 45: Ruth Flanigan.

Math and Science Toolbox: *logos:* Nancy Tobin. 5: Randy Verougstraete. 7–8: Randy Chewning. 10: Randy Verougstraete. *border:* Liisa Chauncy Guida.

Glossary: 10–18: Sharon Hawkins Vargo. 19: Tom Pansini. 20: Sharon Hawkins Vargo.

PHOTOGRAPHS
All photographs by Houghton Mifflin Co. (HMCo.) unless otherwise noted.

Front Cover: *t.* Mark Tomalty/Masterfile Corporation; *m.r.* Craig Tuttle/The Stock Market ; *b.l.* Peter Gridley/FPG International; *b.r.* Tim Davis/Tony Stone Images.

Unit A A: Michael Fogden/DRK Photo. 8–9: George Hunter/Tony Stone Images. 9: *t.* Walter Chandoha; *m.* Darrell Gulin/DRK Photo; *b.* Hans Pfletschinger/Peter Arnold, Inc. 12: *l.* Arthur R. Hill/Visuals Unlimited; *r.* Fritz Polking/Peter Arnold, Inc. 13: Ron Watts/Corbis; *r.* Richard Kolar/Animals Animals/Earth Scenes. 19: D. Demello/Wildlife Conservation Society, Bronx Zoo. 22: *t.l.* © Stephen Collins/Photo Researchers, Inc.; *t.r.* © Thomas Martin/Photo Researchers, Inc.; *b.l.* Darryll Schiff/Tony Stone Images; *b.r.* Zefa Germany/The Stock Market. 23: *t.l.* John M. Roberts/The Stock Market; *t.r.* Thomas Kitchin/Tom Stack & Associates; *b.l.* Thomas Kitchin/Tom Stack & Associates; *b.r.* Brian Parker/Tom Stack & Associates. 24: *t.l.* Stephen J. Krasemann/Tony Stone Images; *t.r.* © Bill Dyer/Photo Researchers, Inc.; *b.l.* Miriam Austerman/Animals Animals/Earth Scenes; *b.r.* Zig Leszczynski/Animals Animals/Earth Scenes. 25: *b.l.* © Tim Davis/Photo Researchers, Inc.; *b.r.* Brian Parker/Tom Stack & Associates. 34: Art Wolfe/Tony Stone Images. 35: S. Purdy Mathews/Tony Stone Images. 36: C. Allen Morgan/Peter Arnold, Inc. 36–37: Stephen Dalton/Animals Animals/Earth Scenes. 37: Michael Fogden/DRK Photo. 40: *t.l.* Sue Streeter/Tony Stone Images; *t.r.* Charles Krebs/Tony Stone Images; *b.l.* Mike Bacon/Tom Stack & Associates; *b.r.* © Gregory Dimijian/Photo Researchers, Inc. 41: *t.l.* Jeanne Drake/Tony Stone Images; *t.r.* © Jim Steingerg/Photo Researchers, Inc.; *b.l.* © Nick Bergkessel/Photo Researchers, Inc.; *b.r.* Fritz Prenzel/Tony Stone Images. 42: *t.l.* Lynn M. Stone/DRK Photo; *r.* E.R. Degginger/Color-Pic, Inc.; *b.l.* © Charles V. Angelo/Photo Researchers, Inc. 43: *l.* Norbert Wu/Tony Stone Images; *r.* Zefa Germany/The Stock Market. 46: *t.l.* Alan G. Nelson/Animals Animals/Earth Scenes; *t.r.* Wayne Lankinen/DRK Photo; *b.* Stephen J. Krasemann/DRK Photo. 47: *t.l.* Tom Lazar/Animals Animals/Earth Scenes; *t.r.* Wayne Lankinen/DRK Photo; *b.* Stephen J. Krasemann/DRK Photo. 50: *t.l.* John Warden/Tony Stone Images; *t.m.* © Treat Davidson/Photo Researchers, Inc.; *t.r.* Stephen J. Krasemann/DRK Photo; *b.l.* © Suzanne L. Collins/Photo Researchers, Inc.; *b.m.* © Jany Sauvanet/Photo Researchers, Inc.; *b.r.* David Northcott/DRK Photo.

Unit B 4–5: *r.* Grant Huntington for HMCo. 14–15: Don & Pat Valenti/DRK Photo. 18–19: Oldrich Karasek/Tony Stone Images. 19: *t.* Tony Freeman/PhotoEdit; *m.* Chris Hackett/The Image Bank; *b.* Wes Thompson/The Stock Market. 20: *m.* © E.R. Degginger/Photo Researchers, Inc.; *b.* © Renee Purse/Photo Researchers, Inc. 21: John P. Kelly/The Image Bank. 24–25: Richard Hutchings for HMCo. 25: Richard Hutchings for HMCo. 26: W. Hille/Leo de Wys. 27: *l.* D. Cavagnaro/DRK Photo; *r.* Superstock. 29: Dwayne Newton/PhotoEdit. 36: Tony Freeman/PhotoEdit. 37: Bob Skjold/PhotoEdit. 40: Hans Reinhard/Bruce Coleman Incorporated. 41: Wayne Lankinen/Bruce Coleman Incorporated. 42: Walter Edwards/National Geographic Society Image Collection. 42.43: S. Nielsen/Imagery. 43: Richard Biegun/FPG International. 46–47: Eric A. Soder/Tom Stack & Associates. 49: Richard Hutchings/PhotoEdit.

Unit C 8–9: Ken Karp for HMCo. 19: *t.* David R. Frazier Photography. 39: *t.* Grant Huntington for HMCo.

Unit D 1: Stephen J. Krasemann/DRK Photo. 18: Tim Davis/Tony Stone Images. 18–19: Wayne Lankinen/DRK Photo. 19: Stephen J. Krasemann/DRK Photo. 24: E.R. Degginger/Color-Pic, Inc. 25: Anne Kuhn/Dwight R. Kuhn. 32: *t.l.* Jerry Jacka Photography; *t.r.* Jerry Jacka Photography. 32–33: David R. Frazier Photography. 33: *t.* David R. Frazier Photography; *b.l.* David R. Frazier Photography; *b.r.* David R. Frazier Photography. 34: *t.l.* E.R. Degginger/Color-Pic, Inc.; *m.r.* E.R. Degginger/Color-Pic, Inc.; *b.l.* E.R. Degginger/Color-Pic, Inc. 35: *r.* Steven Frisch/Stock Boston. 38–39: Superstock. 39: Parvinder S. Sethi. 42–43: Bill Field/Field Photography. 44: *b.l.* Aaron Hahpt/Stock Boston; *b.r.* David Lawrence/The Stock Market.

Unit E E: r. Steven Mark Needham/Envision. 10: Steven Mark Needham/Envision. 10–11: Rick Ostentoski/Envision. 11: Steven Mark Needham/Envision. 16: *t.* Vladimir Morozov/Envision; *b.* Amy Reichman/Envision. 22–23: *inset* Bob Daemmrich Photography. 23: Tim Davis/David Madison Photography. 43: © Catherine Ursillo/Photo Researchers, Inc.